WHAT PEOPLE ARE SAYING ABOUT

SHATTERING THE STAINED GLASS CEILING

. . .

"As a woman and leader in ministry, I understand having an intense desire to accomplish God's purpose and battling opposition to get there. Robyn's message gives great insight into why so many women are struggling to move forward and provides a coaching strategy that will lead them to their breakthrough!"

—Joyce Meyer, Bible teacher and *New York Times* bestselling author of *Battlefield of the Mind*

"I'm deeply passionate about seeing everyone, particularly women, activate the full potential God has placed inside of them. That's why I'm so excited my friend Robyn has written this book *Shattering the Stained Glass Ceiling*. It will challenge and equip you to take hold of the promises God has for you and step up your growth as a woman leader."

—Christine Caine, founder, Propel Women and A21

"Pastor Robyn blessed me tremendously by sharing her leadership and spiritual wisdom when I was preparing to launch a nonprofit ministry. You are now holding Robyn's best counsel! This book is loaded with powerful, barrier-breaking wisdom that she has learned from decades in a thriving, multiministry organization."

—Amy Groeschel, coauthor, *From This Day Forward*

"Having an experienced leader walk alongside you when you are struggling is an invaluable gift. That is exactly what Robyn Wilkerson does in *Shattering the Stained Glass Ceiling*. As an experienced senior pastor and life coach, she has blended her life experiences as a leader with a coaching strategy that will help any leader clarify their path and purpose. I strongly encourage all women leaders to read this book today!"

—Mark Batterson, *New York Times* bestselling author of *The Circle Maker*, lead pastor, National Community Church, Washington DC

"As a professional who has spent her life teaching people how to choose to fully embrace their potential, I highly recommend Robyn Wilkerson's book for women who feel they need a new direction in life and in ministry."

—Caroline Leaf, PhD, cognitive neuroscientist, bestselling author of *Switch on Your Brain*

"Robyn Wilkerson has already navigated a lifetime of uncharted territory in her own personal life with a driven force to succeed beyond what others believe is possible. Now she has created a guide for those who are struggling with identity and purpose, empowering them to exceed the limitations set by their circumstances, and break through to their own success. Robyn's book *Shattering the Stained Glass Ceiling* is that guide, so let's get ready to move forward and prepare for our God-given mandate."

—Joni Lamb, co-founder, Daystar Television Network

"The world needs women to lead gracefully and confidently. In her book *Shattering the Stained Glass Ceiling,* Robyn Wilkerson comes alongside as coach, helping us as we navigate the journey of leadership. Her decades of experience in building the church and her heart to see women fulfill their calling have been inspirational to me. I know this book will help you as you either begin your leadership journey, or take the next step!"

—Holly Wagner, pastor of Oasis Church, author of *Find Your Brave,* founder, GodChicks

"Robyn Wilkerson is an effective ministry leader, and I encourage all women in ministry to read her book *Shattering the Stained Glass Ceiling.* She shares from her life experience and heart the principles that will help you shatter your own stained glass ceiling!"

—Dr. George O. Wood, general superintendent, General Council of the Assemblies of God

"Robyn Wilkerson's book *Shattering the Stained Glass Ceiling* is a must-read for any woman desiring to reach her full potential of balancing gifts, talents, and opportunity. Her transparency and raw authenticity will keep you intrigued; her experience will encourage you; and her principles will instruct you. As entertaining as it is, this book is that and much more—it is a manual of wisdom. Drawing strength from Robyn's life journey will enable you to break every barrier holding you captive as you shatter your personal stained glass ceiling."

—Dr. Alton Garrison, assistant general superintendent, General Council of the Assemblies of God

"I am always thrilled to see resources designed specifically to uplift, guide, and encourage leaders, and Robyn Wilkerson does exactly that in *Shattering the Stained Glass Ceiling*. She not only shares lessons she has learned in her lifetime of ministry leadership, she has developed a coaching strategy designed to jump-start the ministry of any woman leader! Women leaders play an invaluable role in today's church, and I'm certain this book will become a valuable resource to you as you move forward in your leadership role."

—Samuel Rodriguez, president, National Hispanic Christian Leadership Conference, Hispanic Evangelical Association

"*Shattering the Stained Glass Ceiling* guarantees to put into every woman's hand, mind, and heart tools that shatter the stained glass ceiling of ministry success while keeping in perspective the things that matter most to God."

—Sam Farina, DMin, PCC, director, Assemblies of God Coaching

"Maybe it's happened to you one too many times. You have a headache (and honestly, a heartache) from bumping up against the invisible, but absolutely real, overhead barrier that prevents you from reaching your full potential and living out those passionate, Jesus-given dreams to make a difference in this world. Don't despair—help is on the way! In *Shattering the Stained Glass Ceiling*, Robyn Wilkerson offers practical, been-there wisdom and takes a coach approach to hand you the tools to break through your own limitations, whether self-imposed or put there by others. And you know what? Stained glass is pretty, but soaring in the blue skies of possibility is so much better."

—Jodi Detrick, DMin, author of *The Jesus-Hearted Woman*

"For too long women have been programmed to believe they cannot be used in ministry. What God has done for Robyn, He can do in transforming the negatives in women's lives to being positives. I have experienced this in my own life in missionary work in Calcutta, India, and especially after the death of my late husband, Dr. Mark Buntain. As you read the pages of this book, you will find the formula to redirect your life to spiritual fulfillment and a road map to help you find God's direction and purpose for your life in ministry."

—Rev. (Dr.) Huldah Buntain, president/cofounder of the Assemblies of God Mission, Kolkata, India

SHATTERING THE
STAINED GLASS
CEILING

A Coaching Strategy for Women Leaders in Ministry

ROBYN WILKERSON, DMIN

Interior design and formatting by Prodigy Pixel (www.prodigypixel.com)

ISBN: 978-1-68154-059-7

20 19 18 17 • 1 2 3 4

Printed in the United States of America

Every women is a leader because every woman influences someone.

This book is dedicated to all of the wonderful women leaders
who have guided me throughout my life—especially my amazing
mother, Lorraine Buntain, who loved me unconditionally.

And it is dedicated to my sisters, Kathie and Michelle,
to my daughters-in-love Ashley, DawnCheré, and Kristen,
and to my darling granddaughters, Israel and Nora,
who are my inspiration.

This book was only possible thanks to the support of my
husband, Richard, who pushed me to keep going. Thank you,
darling, for being you! I love you!

CONTENTS

PREFACE

The fact that I am a woman does not make me a different kind of Christian, but the fact that I am a Christian does make me a different kind of woman.

—ELISABETH ELLIOT

I love the ocean. Right now the sound of the icy Alaskan waves hitting the side of our cruise ship is a calming rhythm. It's the perfect setting to write. Perched on our portside balcony, I'm gazing across the endless gray ocean into a misty horizon, with the perfect brisk chill stimulating my mind. Yep. This is home.

Having been raised in the Pacific Northwest, this rainy, cold foggy day is my vibe. Somewhere I was told that one of the reasons people love the sea is due to a naturally occurring antidepressant effect as salt water ions evaporate from its surface.

Well, whatever the reasons are, the outcome is always the same for me: I'm at peace when I'm near the ocean. The endless waves and untold depths of uncharted expanse are a powerful metaphor to me of God's limitless universe.

I like to think there's a sea in all of us. Your internal mental world, which we can correlate to an ocean, is the deep, wonderfully rich composite of you, filled with your thoughts, feelings, memories, dreams, hopes, and desires. However, it can also be filled with storms of inadequacy, insecurity, regrets, fears, disappointment, and hopelessness. We've all felt this inner sea crash in on us, threatening to drown our future.

Today my prayer is "Father, Your ocean is so big, and my boat is so small!" So often it can feel that my capacity is fragile and small. My endurance leaks, and my world begins to feel as though I will sink—but I never have. God always comes through. Just in time!

Here is why I wrote this book for you: Godly women with untapped leadership potential are standing on the sidelines, and it's time for them to get into the game. We women have been quick to blame our lack of leadership on men, but they aren't holding us back. We are.

We aren't men, and we need to stop thinking our leadership needs to look the same. There is no one-size-fits-all version of effective leadership in a ministry context. Eleanor Roosevelt said, "No one can make you feel inferior without your consent." Don't give your consent!

It's time to disrupt and recreate the model of women in ministry leadership. We must challenge previous notions of what effective ministry looks like. Dear friend, you can be everything God has created and called you to be. Being a woman isn't an obstacle to your leadership—it's your asset!

You might be thinking it's too late for you. But God is a God of second chances and fresh starts. Since you are alive, breathing, and reading this book, God obviously isn't finished with you yet. Don't quit, and don't give up, even when you've experienced failure. Instead, allow God to use failure to move you forward.

Are you ready to have a shift happen in one or more areas of your life? Do you feel stuck? Do you lack clarity, direction, and accountability? Do you crave more meaning and fulfillment in your life but aren't quite sure how to access it? Then the leadership coaching strategy of this book is for you.

You are certain to gain new, profound insights about how to get out of your own way. You'll discover practical tools to take your personal life and ministry to a level of unlimited possibilities! This coaching strategy equips you to:

1. *Integrate* spirituality into the practice of your leadership.
2. *Assess* leadership attributes both in yourself and others.
3. *Articulate* a statement of personal mission and goals.
4. *Plan* a consistent program of leadership self-development.
5. *Monitor* your interior life for signs of growth and health, and be able

to intervene to correct deficiencies.

6. *Describe* understanding of your essential leadership attributes and why they are important.

7. *Prepare* for greater ministry effectiveness by building your core strengths from the inside out.

It's time to step up to the front of the crowd and say, "Here I am! I'm ready to serve and to lead!"

CHAPTER ONE

REACHING YOUR FULL POTENTIAL

Eve was created to know and walk with God and to make Him known to others by reflecting His character in her life. This is a woman's true path to fulfillment and meaning—the only way we will ever discover who we are and find our purpose. And it is accessible to all of us.

—CAROLYN CUSTIS JAMES

"I'm stuck."

As she dramatically fell back into the patio couch, Haley shook her head back and forth, saying again, *"I am stuck!"*

"What are you talking about?"

"I'm stuck. I can't get going in anything! One year ago today I was exactly where I am today! I'm stuck in every part of my life. My ministry is going nowhere. My family life is full of chaos. I hate how I look! I feel awful. I'm sick and tired of being sick and tired . . . but I don't know what to do to change!"

I let her frustrated words hang in the air, allowing her dramatic moment to sink in. Part of me wanted to contradict her, but a larger part of me agreed with her. She was absolutely right!

One year earlier, she had come to me about her dissatisfaction. She wanted a boyfriend with the hope to be married one day. She had finished college, but she felt she needed more specialized training for her professional life to move forward. She was overweight, not in good shape, and she really wanted to get fit. Her ministry with her church wasn't growing.

Haley envisioned herself as a public speaker, teaching and mentoring other young women; instead she was doing data entry and setting up tables. After a full year, she had not managed to attract volunteer team members to elevate her ministry department at her church. She was underpaid and couldn't implement her creative plans for fund-raising. Bottom line, after one year she had not made progress in any area of her life. So what could I say to help this sharp young leader deal with a moment of truth in her ministry, her family, and her personal life?

Does Haley's story sound familiar? Do you share her situation? Are you stuck? The wonderful news is I had an answer for her, and I have the same answer for you: *You can change!*

WHAT IS A STAINED GLASS CEILING?

Throughout this book, I refer to the "stained glass ceiling," so I want to make sure you understand exactly what I mean by the term. Here are some definitions to help us get started:

- *Stained glass ceiling* is a term used to describe the unseen, often perceived as unbreakable, barrier that prevents women from rising to accept their full ministry calling regardless of their qualifications or achievements. It's formally defined as "any barrier to the advancement of women within church leadership; also, by extension, a barrier to women in other fields on the basis of religious beliefs."[1] The phrase "stained glass" refers to the traditional placement of stained glass windows in places of Christian worship.
- *Glass ceiling* is defined as an "invisible but real barrier through which the next stage or level of advancement can be seen but cannot be reached by a section of qualified and deserving employees. Such barriers exist due to implicit prejudice on the basis of age, ethnicity, political or religious affiliation, and/or sex. Although generally illegal, such practices are prevalent in most countries."[2] The term is typically attributed to Gay Bryant who

used it in interviews and in the book *The Working Woman Report: Succeeding in Business in the 1980s* (1984). However, who initially used it and when is debated.[3]

- *Glass cliff* "is a concept first identified by Michelle K. Ryan and S. Alexander Haslam in a 2005 paper and documented in dozens of studies since. It describes situations where women executives can be set up to work under conditions that lead to job dissatisfaction, feelings of disempowerment, and higher turnover."[4]

SHATTERING YOUR STAINED GLASS CEILING

Countless women leaders around the world have already smashed the *stained glass ceiling*. It is happening today as women of every age, color, and culture break through into frontiers of uncharted territory, pursuing personal and professional accomplishment. To elevate their futures, women leaders of faith are pioneering new roads by activating the unlimited potential of their gifts and talents. They are tearing down barriers that previous generations of women could never have imagined!

For any woman to shatter the stained glass ceiling, she must not only possess the qualities of preparation, character, skill, and leadership, but she must be willing to sharpen her capacity and increase her growth. As women, I believe the time has passed to look for reasons why our leadership might be marginalized based on our ethnicity or gender. Instead, we must grab hold of exciting new global opportunities by preparing ourselves for marketplace ministry leadership. To accomplish our mission, we must take hold of the responsibilities of personal development and the disciplines of spiritual formation. By leveraging our strengths, we can step into places of leadership—without reservation!

So how can a woman who is serving in a ministry context cultivate her leadership calling? As a third-generation pastor, and now with my four sons and their wives all serving as pastors, this urgent question has shaped my commitment to this project. Around the world, the organizations and churches that are experiencing the greatest success are those that have

Our world is in desperate need of your unique leadership, which God predestined to blend into your one-of-a-kind feminine identity.

opened their cultures to the full humanity of women, including the leadership of women. Whether your ministry is in the church, on the missions field, in a classroom, working in an office, or within the walls of your home, your leadership is valuable!

There is no time to lose. Our world is in desperate need of your unique leadership, which God predestined to blend into your one-of-a-kind feminine identity. Communities, organizations, churches, families, and individuals (many unborn) are waiting for your divinely inspired leadership to help them soar to their highest potential. You must purposefully build your capacity to lead— beginning now! The coaching strategy in this book can help you achieve amazing success as you increase your leadership skills. Now is your time to break through into your divine destiny. Today is your opportunity!

YOUR MISSION IS YOUR LEGACY

Your mission, your calling, is bigger than you. This is what I know about you if you are a Christian woman desiring to activate God's call in your life: You are ready to work hard to see your calling from God become reality. *You aren't alone!*

All over the world, Christian women leaders in ministry are standing in kitchens ladling hot food for the poor. They are sacrificing time and money to reach out to distressed single parents and displaced immigrant families. Leaders are found in every walk of life, from the boardroom to the battlefield. They are serving in hospitals, prisons, schools, homes, communities, churches, neighborhoods, businesses, and government. They are leaving lucrative careers to launch organizations and churches that provide aid and spiritual renewal to millions.

Christian women leaders are serving in unspeakable environments, against impossible obstacles, to fulfill their callings. God has given us eyes to see, hearts to love, hands to tend, and we want to offer these hearts and hands back to God for all He has accomplished for us and in us. You aren't motivated by power or money, but by the desire to make your life count. At the end of your journey on earth, you want to know that your life wasn't in vain, that your days were not swallowed up by the tide of human history. You agree with Tolkien, "No half-heartedness and no worldly fear must turn us aside from following the light unflinchingly."

All over the world, women just like you are taking practical steps to understand their calling. They are finding new ways to create a more positive understanding of their leadership skills and to bring greater value to their organization or church. Women leaders are working to deepen their loyalty to themselves and their cause, and to build stronger, enduring long-term relationships for the future. All over the world, women leaders are also looking for new ways to enjoy their work more fully, to get along with congregants and teams more easily, and to feel better about themselves. The pathway for achieving these professional and personal goals is through a clearer comprehension of your leadership approach and understanding how you can gain deeper traction for better results.

When we take on challenges, we wrestle with a degree of uncertainty, and we risk failure. We risk losing. We risk getting hurt. However, fail or succeed, by doing risky things we expand our vision of what is possible. Every effort builds our character and equips us with the skills, the confidence, and the essential attributes needed to navigate the obstacles we face.

You have unlimited potential. God wants to do amazing things in your life as you open up your thinking. By gaining awareness of the history of sacrifice and service of the Christian women who have gone before you, and by valuing those young women leaders who are coming behind you, you can reduce your isolation and capture the positive energy you need to spring into action and engage in social connection to other women.

It isn't enough for me to tell you stories of Christian women leaders who dared to break through the stained glass ceiling of leadership to overcome hardship and create eternal transformation outcomes in the lives of those they served. You must grab this revelation for yourself and believe that you are a leader. Let's begin with this truth: *Your life matters.*

- *God has a purpose for everyone.* "But I have raised you up for this very purpose, that I might show you my power and that my name might be proclaimed in all the earth" (Ex. 9:16).
- *You are gifted and called.* "The purposes of a person's heart are deep waters, but one who has insight draws them out" (Prov. 20:5).
- *You are needed.* "Therefore, my dear friends, as you have always obeyed—not only in my presence, but now much more in my absence—continue to work out your salvation with fear and trembling, for it is God who works in you to will and to act in order to fulfill his good purpose" (Phil. 2:12–13).

SO WHAT IS COACHING?

Coaching is a powerful tool that guides you as you move forward from where you are in your life to where you want to go—change. It will help you articulate your visionary plan for your leadership in a way that's compelling, measurable, and marked by stunning clarity.[5] Imagine that the role of coaching in your leadership is like a machete. When it is skillfully engaged in a forest of dense foliage and underbrush, it makes a path clear. It removes obstacles.

Coaching broadens your path for others to follow. It empowers greater accomplishment of your goals. Most leaders regularly pick up this concept of coaching, but quickly put it back down because they aren't trained to use it properly. Others keep swinging like crazy, unaware their machete is dull. Then, after much hard work with little results, they become frustrated and confused with failure. This book examines how to sharpen your machete by applying coaching to your leadership skills.

Life is a journey full of obstacles and opportunities to make decisions that will impact our destinies. Our personal life story is tied to the basic human instinct to reach for more. Every human shares the drive to create abundance in every area of life. Within the process of creation, an individual can often achieve a sense of purpose and satisfaction. Self-worth rises as we look forward to a positive, personal plan to engage the future with passion and creativity. At our deepest level, we view life with the hope of improving ourselves and our communities.

The Genesis narrative of God's first act of creation describes Him speaking order into chaos, with each succeeding day revealing a new aspect of His development of creation (Gen. 1 and 2). God spoke into existence an improved reality as He organized the cosmos. He created the earth, then the animal kingdoms, and finally His prized creation of humankind. God set a precedent of continued improvement moving forward in time.

Adam and Eve lived in a perfect paradise in close relationship with God and with each other. However, they rebelled in spite of this paradise existence. God forced them out of Eden, and they found themselves standing outside their home, facing the consequences of their toxic thinking. Adam and Eve were stuck.

Since that moment, every human has faced uncertain tomorrows. With that first expulsion from Eden, our lives on earth became a never-ending struggle for physical survival and an existential longing to reconnect to a higher way of living—an inner human longing for something more. Our strong inner drive for meaning and purpose simply proves meaning and purpose do exist!

This perception of improving compels us to strive forward, toward a deeper connection to God, a better community with others, clearer expressions of vocation, more effective use of time and resources, healthier lifestyle habits, and developed skills. However, the individual's personal pursuit of improving doesn't always go well. We can become lazy or exhausted, disappointed or depressed. Obstacles overwhelm us, and then the pressure to make decisions sidelines progress and swamps us.

Just like Adam and Eve, we all get stuck, but coaching can help us reach beyond that to our full potential. The goal of this book is to coach you forward by helping you improve in every area of your life, especially in your leadership capacity and ministry.

> Life is a journey full of obstacles and opportunities to make decisions that will impact our destinies.

GETTING OUT OF THE RUT

To get out of the rut and move your life to the next level, you need to understand the external world is not the driving force for who you become or what you choose to create for your life. You control your thinking, and that shapes the direction of your life. By taking control of your thinking, you move toward fully developing your emotional, physical, financial, and spiritual potential.

If you want to change your life, you must change your thinking. Why do achievement and success seem like a possibility to one person but impossible to someone else in the same situation? I'm a pastor and a life coach. I've studied many hard-working women, especially those working in ministry roles. Through my years of observation, it's become clear why some women leaders thrive while others, in the same situation, become stuck in hopelessness. The difference is found in perception. How a woman sees her situation—with all its obstacles and opportunities—is the key to her personal success. Although it could be argued that most of these women's lives are parallel in potential, preparation, and even drive, when I dug deeper I could identify that they were actually living in different realities.

Some women leaders in ministry live in a reality in which success seems possible, despite obvious obstacles. Others are stuck in a reality where success seems impossible. No matter how many hours of coaching I might invest, a woman can't expect to achieve success if she lives frozen in a mind-set that change is impossible. Being stuck in life means she is stuck in her thinking. As a coach, I understand that if we want to create long-term, sustainable, transformational change in women leaders' lives, we must help them shift their reality by changing how they view their world. Before potential, there is motivation. Before motivation, there is emotion. Before emotion, there is reality.

How you think *is* your reality—it is the difference between a burst of new resolutions that fail before they start and a permanent mind-set that promotes success in every personal and professional endeavor. To create a positive change in your life, you first have to change your personal inner reality: *You have to change your thinking.* Life is now. It's never too late or too early. Right now is a good time for change if you want to move from where you are to where you want to be!

THINGS TO CONSIDER:

1. What barriers are you facing in your life and ministry that you would like to break through?

   lack of self-confidence, constant worry, uncertainty of the future/where I should go.

2. What positive steps can you take right now to cultivate your leadership calling?

   Be more kind to myself emotionally, mentally, physically

3. You have unlimited potential! What legacy would you like to leave for those coming after you?

   More women and men knowing & pursuing God's full purpose for their lives.

4. What are three ways coaching could help you move forward in breaking those barriers and cultivating your leadership calling?

   - have a healthier mindset about myself
   - stop blaming others/worrying about others
   - have tangible goals

5. Look at your answers to the previous questions. How could changing your perception about your barriers help you move forward in your life and ministry?

CHAPTER TWO

MY LEADERSHIP JOURNEY

The deepest experience of the creator is feminine—:for it is experience of receiving and bearing.

—RAINER MARIA RILKE

"What am I here for? What is my purpose?" Millions of women have asked these questions. Back when I was a pig-tailed, chubby girl in grade school, if you had asked me what I wanted to be when I grew up I would likely have responded with a big smile and answered something like a mommy or a teacher. Becoming a pastor to a large, ethnic, urban congregation, leading a social service agency with millions of dollars of government funding, and preaching on television and radio would never have crossed my mind. Traveling around the world meeting famous persons of influence and living in a community with residents whose names are on the front pages of leading newspapers was outside my imagination as well. I had no idea where my life would take me. I could never have imagined where God's purposes for my life would lead.

"Life without purpose and passion is a life not worth living."[1] We need to find our passion, the spark that keeps us motivated and moving. Many women live with indifference, fatigue, and dissatisfaction. For them, life is a never-ending cycle of laundry, dishes, holidays, obligations, and responsibilities. Years and years of oppressive thinking continue to hold back their spiritual development and progress.[2]

So what is the answer? How can we find passion for life? What is our purpose on planet earth? The answer is simple. We are here to enjoy God and to do His will.[3] We were created for His pleasure. God, who created

> God's purpose for our lives unfolds in front of us as we let go of our plans and step into His plan.

the universe, expressed His will to dwell in and among us. Paul wrote, we "are being built together for a dwelling place of God in the Spirit" (Eph. 2:22, NKJV). So often we want to know what God is going to do *for us*, rather than asking what God wants to do *through us*. God's purpose for each of us is where our destiny can be fulfilled. Knowing we are fulfilling our God-given purpose is the only way to ignite and sustain true passion.[4]

Passion, the zeal or enthusiasm for life, is the gasoline of the soul. Knowing we are living God's purpose for our lives sets us free to let go and let God work things out His way. The Bible says in Romans 11:33 (AMPC) that God's ways, methods, and paths are "unfathomable."

However, we also know there is a purpose in everything God does. "The LORD has made everything [to accommodate itself and contribute] to its own end and His own purpose" (Prov. 16:4, AMPC). God's purpose for our lives unfolds in front of us as we let go of our plans and step into His plan. Our lack of passion is a result of our own unmet expectations for how life is turning out. We make big plans for our lives. We tell God what we want and how we want it. When He chooses to continue to work His purposes in us and we don't get what we've asked for, we get frustrated, confused, and angry. We need to give ourselves permission not to know and to be satisfied knowing the One who does.[5]

We will never enjoy life until we accept God's will with joy and stop trying to understand everything that happens contrary to our own desires. If we stop trusting our own ideas of how our lives should be going, the Bible promises our health and energy will increase! "Don't be conceited, sure of your own wisdom. Instead, trust and reverence the LORD, and turn your back on evil; when you do that, then you will be given renewed health and vitality" (Prov. 3:7, TLB).

FINDING MYSELF

My biggest barrier to breakthrough is my temptation to ask over and over, "Why, God? Why is my life going this way? Why did You let that happen to me?" Nothing can hold me back from spiritual growth and cut off my spiritual passion faster than questioning and complaining to God and to everyone around me. Accepting the simple truth that I *don't* know why God allows stuff to happen, and being satisfied with knowing that only He knows why, is where my passion for living is regenerated. Passion is restored inside trust.

This hasn't been an easy lesson for me to learn. I keep facing the same barrier over and over. Understanding why I do what I do in every part of my life is an exercise in self-analysis. It requires careful thought and personal reflection on my emotional, psychological, and spiritual development. Being aware of how that developmental journey integrates with my identity, faith experience, psychological development, and life experiences is paramount to having a better understanding of my inner self.[6]

My earliest memory is happily dancing in my sun-filled bedroom to music playing from my record player. I was dressed in a pink, satin ballet suit, enjoying myself in our Oakland, California, parsonage. I couldn't have been more than three years old, but my memories are packed with a sense of joy, love, and security. My parents were very loving. They loved God, each other, and their family. We had a happy life. My dad was a warm, affirming father, and my mom was ever steady, always ready with the solution to every situation. Inside our house and church, I felt solid. I felt strong and smart. I was invincible. But as I began to grow, it didn't stay that way.

Culture impacted me. The Hippie Movement was just getting started. The Beatles had broken every sales record, and screaming crowds followed them everywhere. A powerful youth revolution had begun, and with this open rebellion to establishment came the unbridled use of drugs, communal living, and self-gratification. I was thirteen years old when college and high school students began streaming into San Francisco for the infamous "Summer of Love."[7] Living in Southern California heightened the peer pressure to be identified with the new trend. Teenagers dressed, talked, sang, and acted out a whole new set of values that astonished the older generation.

At that time, my parents accepted a pastorate in the Pacific Northwest, extracting my siblings and me from the negative tsunami of pop culture. At seventeen, as I graduated from Woodrow Wilson High School, I was totally confused about what a woman's role was supposed to be. Women's liberation was the mantra of the hour. I didn't have any reason to think women hadn't always been free, but my friends seemed to see it differently. My closest girlfriends rushed into unrestricted sexual expression, anti-marriage relationships, and began a lifelong pursuit of professional career goals outside of the home. My generation strongly rejected classic roles and became intensely intolerant of those young women who opted to choose traditional lifestyles.

Becoming a Christian spiritual leader was the last role a hip, relevant, young woman would ever have considered. In spite of my inner calling, it sounded preposterous to think about ministry or even "square Christian living" as a serious career path for a woman. Although my outward appearance suggested I was in agreement with the popular youth rebellion, I knew I was going to walk into my destiny of spiritual leadership in ministry.

At six years old, inside my father's church, my Sunday school teacher led me in the sinner's prayer. Katherine Kuhlman was a famous televangelist at that time and my teacher, Miss Geneva Dixon, was her sister. Geneva explained the plan of salvation to our small class, and I answered the call. I felt destiny was guiding me, and God had equipped me to accomplish great things for Him. At twelve years old, under the ministry of Gladys Pearson, I received the baptism in the Holy Spirit with the evidence of speaking in tongues. From those moments until now, I've always carried a sense of purpose. That sense of calling has overshadowed every decision I've made.

My friends thought it was a shocking decision to drop out of college to marry my youth pastor boyfriend. I prayed and prayed about that decision, and I had the strongest impression that if I didn't marry Rich, I would be going against God's plan for my life. My impression while praying at the altar in my father's church was that God had a strong purpose for me to fulfill, and I could do it the easy way or the hard way. I chose what I thought would be the easy way and quickly made plans to get married. My radical decision was deeply grounded in my sense of calling. I was nineteen.

Marrying Rich Wilkerson was my surest tether to my spiritual inner voice, but being a wife and functioning inside the church as a pastor in 1973 wasn't easy. I tried hard to be included, but as the journey unfolded I

> I had the strongest impression that if I didn't marry Rich, I would be going against God's plan for my life.

felt marginalized and irrelevant—certainly unimportant. For me, there was no ministry leadership path inside the church. Receiving a salary or a job description for any work I did on behalf of my husband's ministry was never a serious consideration from any of the leaders in the churches we served. As a woman, I could find no mentors or peers who were flourishing as leaders inside the church. Conflict began inside my own thinking. Who was I supposed to emulate? Where were women who were actually leading inside the church? Unable to sing solos, and unwilling to become a custodian or secretary, the conflict between myself and my husband heated up. He held a clear picture of what a pastor's wife should be, but I was a liberated Christian woman and was shocked to discover that equality for female leadership within the church was only a concept. I knew I had been called to spiritual leadership but finding a pathway to my goal seemed impossible.

Within commonplace routine, mundane challenges churned out endless opportunities for me to be tested and to grow in faith. God was always present, quietly nudging me. Time brought the births of four sons, and the daily routine of caring for children. Building a home and family of excellence, it turned out, was much harder than I had anticipated. Daily routines of meals, laundry, and homework became the terrain where my emotional muscles of perseverance, patience, and self-control were tested and perfected.

Then my life changed. Our third son, Graham, was stricken with spinal meningitis at six months old, and inside that terrible tragedy God volunteered me to become the mother of a child with a handicap. I thought I would explode. Graham was very delayed in his development. He struggled and struggled. Years of uphill challenges, including Graham's tantrums, medication, doctors, therapists, special education costs, and never-ending behavior problems put me into a rage. Furious with God for letting me down, and for not healing Graham the way I requested, I quit praying. We all did the best we could to cope. Our marriage was extremely tested. No matter which direction I tried to go, I felt trapped.

My faith in God went through the wringer. This single event in Graham's life became the defining turning point of my young adulthood. I had never before been summoned to face any obstacle of this magnitude. Denial, begging, and rage became my constant conversation with God. *Why me? Why did I have to be a mom to a special needs child? What have I done to deserve this prison of broken dreams? How will I ever rise above my circumstances to fulfill the mission God has placed in my heart?*

Leonard Sweet writes,

> To put it bluntly: the whole leadership thing is a demented concept. Leaders are neither born nor made. Leaders are summoned. They are called into existence by circumstances. Those who rise to the occasion are leaders. Everyone is 'called' by God for some kind of mission. But sometimes the 'called' are 'called out' for leadership. How you manifest your mission will change throughout the course of your life. But the mission remains constant.[8]

I wasn't born a leader. I certainly didn't volunteer to be the mom of a special needs child, but my situation summoned me. I had to become a leader to answer "the call," which I had to choose to believe God had allowed into my life. Today, Graham is a strong healthy young adult who loves his family and works hard to serve his church. He walks, talks, runs a computer, has his driver's license, and well . . . frankly, he's a powerful personality. No, Graham will probably never live on his own, but he's the light of our family. Being Graham's mom has been the highest privilege of my life and my hardest mission. Because of Graham, I've been taught faith, courage, resilience, perseverance, gratitude, acceptance, and love. No, I still wouldn't volunteer to be a special-needs mother, but in God's eternal economy He had untold blessings waiting for me on the other side of my heartbreak.

The worst thing that ever happened to me eventually became the best thing—ever. How will you rise to the occasion in your life? Will you be there when life calls you forth to be a warrior? Will you answer the call of the "called-forth" leadership?[9] The truth is no matter what you face, God has already equipped and resourced you with *everything* you need to fight the battle and win your war. The only question you have to answer is will you say yes.

Today, thirty years later, I see that in every life situation, another subplot was unfolding in my life. Our community and family never let go of me, or of Graham. My parents, siblings, and church community stood by us calmly— every step of the way. God was using this terrible illness to press all of us into different people. My husband, my boys, and I were no longer the picture-perfect family. Now we were needy. We couldn't fix Graham without God.

Watching the struggles of little Graham opened all our eyes to the needs of kids just like him everywhere. Our church allowed me to open a special education program within our Christian school, and years later hundreds have benefited and found educational success. Living with the frustrations and disappointments of Graham's disabilities created sensitivity in the hearts of our other three sons for people who aren't accepted by society as "first string." Watching the heartbreak of handicap expanded their understanding, empathy, and nonjudgmental acceptance of others. This molding force set our other three sons up to become better humans. They became more patient, more calm, and stronger than other boys their age. Under adversity and inside disappointment for Graham's physical impairments, our boys acquired a kinder, gentler endurance then I could ever have imagined. Little did I know that God's purpose in their lives was being forged in their hearts, preparing them for our next test.

The worst
thing
that ever
happened
to me
eventually
became
the best
thing—ever.

A NEW KIND OF MINISTRY

In 1998, my evangelist husband announced to me and the boys that he was called to pastor in urban Miami. After months of conversation, we uprooted our brood from suburban America to an ethnic, inner-city ministry. Rich was energized to step into his new leadership role as an inner-city pastor. Our boys experienced a huge identity crisis and cultural trauma. Conflict emerged with a bang! Every part of our spiritual leadership was tested in a new set of circumstances—poverty, lack, and religious tradition.

My husband's call to spiritual leadership tested our commitment to each other and to our identity as a ministry family. The drama of stepping into a deprived, ethnic culture, struggling to reestablish community in Miami, and pushing forward in the commonplace daily routine seemed impossible. I desperately wanted to go back to Tacoma, but our call strengthened our resolve to stay.

God was in the daily details. Every morning, hungry people stood waiting for help in our church parking lot. Our campus was insect- and rodent-infested. The church lacked everything from scissors to a sound system. I didn't want to do the tasks that needed to be done. I didn't want to be a pastor for this city. I was in a rage again. The truth is, when I didn't understand why circumstances came into my life that were painful or difficult, I got angry with God. But His purposes are always working out in our lives, and as the months rolled on I could see that no matter how loudly I complained, His consistent guiding presence always made it clear what needed to be done next. I never wondered what to do, *I just didn't want to do it!*

Inside the routine administration of building a faith community, God transformed me into a senior pastor. Rich was constantly traveling to raise funds for the church ministry. We hired several professional associate pastors, thinking they would shoulder the pastoral leadership burden. They tried, and their families made every effort to fit into the congregation, but the cultural divide was simply too enormous.

The same month the associate pastors decided to leave, a hurricane destroyed our tent auditorium. Our growing congregation had to move back into tight quarters. Then came the biggest challenge: Rich suffered compartment syndrome in his leg and came close to needing an amputation. He was in a wheelchair, which meant I had to step up and lead. I had no choice. God had a purpose He was working out in my life and in the lives of my boys. I knew what to do, *but I didn't want to do it.*

Asking God *why* only intensified the challenge. The truth is, I am a spiritual leader. I was called to leadership in the basement of my Sunday school class years earlier. Since then, I had learned the critical leadership skills I would need to serve as a lead pastor in an urban setting. Openness to people came from struggling to cope with the differences of children like my Graham. Patience and calmness when facing Graham's raging tantrums grew inside me. Perseverance developed in my heart in the face of impossible outcomes while sitting in countless doctors' offices only to get their negative prognosis. Years of working and believing for Graham's physical healing in the face of overwhelming odds steeled fierce faith into my character. These same lessons were learned by my other three sons.

Communion with God and recognizing His unmistakable fingerprint on every challenge carried us through. The forces of conflict, coupled with communion, community, and the commonplace routine of doing what God sets in front of you is His pathway to shaping the hearts of spiritual leaders to fulfill their designed destiny. I made my first profession of faith under the ministry of two women—spiritual leaders! God has been weaving a leadership story all the way through my life!

GOD'S PLAN IS BEST

As a Christian leader, it's vital to have a solid understanding of your current self and who God intends for you to become. You need to be aware of the importance and interplay of wholeness and holiness to have a sense

> We begin our spiritual relationship with God at the point of His holiness.

of direction in life. God declares, "So set yourselves apart to be holy, for I am the LORD your God" (Lev. 20:7, NLT). To set ourselves apart is to refuse a relationship with the world. James clearly states to believers in the new covenant, "If you want to be a friend of the world, you make yourself an enemy of God" (James 4:4, NLT).[10]

We begin our spiritual relationship with God at the point of His holiness. James taught that we must choose to set ourselves apart; being holy is not an option. God will not dwell in us and among us if we fail to separate ourselves from the world system. However, we aren't God. We were created in human bodies that deteriorate, and we have personalities that often suffer from periods of emotional stress or a dark side. Striving toward a positive lifestyle of holiness, while mitigating the negative effects of our dark side, is the battle every honest, adult Christian must face.[11]

Recognizing that personal dysfunction exists in every human being to some degree, we must be willing to stay accountable to God by accepting the scrutiny of others into our private and public lives.[12] I know; it can be an uncomfortable thought. How does this play out in real life? It means staying fully engaged in family and personal relationships no matter how misunderstood we feel. Or it might mean persevering inside organizational reproof or negative performance assessments. A mature personality has a solid sense of self, which is anchored in a strong foundation of self-worth. This is always the result of healthy personality development. Tests, challenges, staying accountable, and accepting authority are all part of what every adult must grapple with to push forward in personal spiritual growth.

I know you want to live a satisfying life as much as I do. As we strive to better ourselves and achieve our goals, it can be frustrating to watch other people enjoying life as we struggle. God wants us to live the good life![13] We must begin our Christian life believing not only that His purpose is good for us, but that *His plan is best for us*. The key to finding fulfillment is sustaining passion for life, and the key to sustaining passion is trusting in God's purposes even when we don't understand why.

THINGS TO CONSIDER:

1. What does God want to do through you? What role has He called you to fulfill?

    - Career-wise, I'm not sure, except to mentor/teach college students about living a holy life
    - Other main roles: wife, daughter, friend

2. How have the trials you have faced in life prepared you to fulfill God's call on your life?

    - Marriage difficulties: advice/wisdom for others
    - Growing up issues and work experiences have given me patience, search for real truth/joy

3. What obstacles have you faced or are currently facing that are preventing you from fulfilling your call?

    - Rejection from others makes me feel inadequate

4. How do you personally need to change to move forward in fulfilling your call? (leadership skills, training, self-esteem, health, etc.)

    - Self-esteem most definitely!
    - Training/searching what roles God is guiding me into for the future.

5. What can you do to help yourself trust in God's purposes for your life even when you don't understand the "why"?

    - Remain patient and content no matter the circumstances
    - Remember when all seemed lost how God worked through it all.

CHAPTER THREE

FIVE ESSENTIAL LEADERSHIP ATTRIBUTES

If I never got to make a living doing what I loved, I'd still do it—for fun and for free.

—SUSAN E. ISAACS

"Get out of bed, Robyn! For heaven's sake, why are you still in that bed? This is the third time I've called you, and it's the last time. If you don't get up, I'm coming in there to get you up myself!"

I was exhausted, and the last thing I wanted to do was get up early and go, so in my whiny voice I answered, "Mom, why won't you just leave me alone? I don't want to go!" As the sleep fell away from my consciousness, I struggled to sit up and pull myself out of bed. This time, I shouted down the hall so she could hear me, "Hey, Mom, here's a question. Why do I have to go to church again?"

Before I could get to my feet, my little, five-foot Norwegian mom bounded into my room, laughing, and roared at me, "Because you're the pastor! That's why! Now get ready!" Mom was visiting us in Miami, and I was late for church.

I understand women leaders in ministry. I get them. As a third-generation woman pastor, I've lived the calling. Waking up every day of my entire life, believing God has chosen me to work in ministry, has been the foundation of my life. I've lived the thrill of facing insurmountable challenges and I've enjoyed the satisfaction of seeing eternal results in the lives of the people I serve.

THE CALL TO LEADERSHIP

Being a woman in ministry isn't a job, it's a lifestyle. There has never been one moment in my life when I didn't measure my behavior by the standard of upholding the expectations for women in church leadership. Every piece of clothing or jewelry I've worn, every restaurant I've eaten in, every friendship I've nurtured, every association I've forged, every song I've listened to, every book I've read, every movie I've seen, every word I've spoken, and every thought I've embraced have all been measured by my understanding of what was expected of women in ministry.

These expectations weren't just for the women who were employed by a church or ministry organization, but for all Christian women leaders serving in a ministry context. Although it might sound like a burden to many, this way of thinking has been a clear pathway in my life and has brought tremendous security to my identity. Yes, like every young person I had seasons of wanting to run in the other direction from my parents, my church life, and my ministry obligations, but being a Christian woman leader has been an enormously satisfying and successful way of life for me.

One thing I know for sure is the world desperately needs leadership. Visit any news station and you'll recognize our cultural crisis in abandoned values, betrayed trust, manipulation, and sheer exploitation. Corporate leaders exploit the privileges of position and bring devastation to the lives of their investors, employees, and customers. Church leaders experience lapses of integrity, compromising and marginalizing their congregations, and seeding disillusionment and cynicism. Families and personal relationships dissolve from covenant while crashing over the edge into conflict-ridden courtroom battles.

We see self-serving leaders promoting pride and self-protecting leaders promoting fear across every sphere of our religious, business, education, government, medical, and military institutions. Many leaders behave as if the sheep were only there for the benefit of the shepherd. That's the bad news. The good news is there's a better way, and your leadership can help us get there!

So what is leadership? It's a process of influence.[1] Leadership expert Peter Drucker defined a leader as someone who has followers. As a leader, you need to understand, "Leadership is the capacity to translate vision into reality."[2] Vision is vital to your leadership, as is your ability to empower others.[3] As a leader, you use your social influence to maximize the efforts of others, moving them toward the achievement of a goal.[4]

Within the context of their ministry, women leaders must engage in a new kind of leadership—"transformissional" leadership.[5] Coined by Steve Ogne and Tim Roehl, the phrase *transformissional leadership* refers to leaders who express and engage the Great Commission. Coaching is a valuable part of this process because, "Great coaches come alongside leaders so that leaders can be transformed into the image of Christ and join Him in His redemptive mission."[6]

The most effective women leaders are "transformissional" leaders. These women leaders create an inspiring vision of the future, which motivates and inspires people to engage with that vision.[7] They manage the delivery of the vision as they coach their teams for greater capacity to achieve the vision. "Transformissional" leadership brings together the skills needed to do these things.

Leadership is an exceptional gift, isn't it? Great women leaders aren't just born; they develop by building on the lessons of their times. Every woman who is willing to learn and to extract wisdom from life's transformative moments can grow to become a more effective leader. When a woman leader models effective, "transformissional" leadership, it's a continuous process of influence that changes people's thinking, behavior, or development toward accomplishing a goal in their personal or professional lives.[8]

"Leadership is always about character."[9] Some situations we experience in life will either crush us or inspire us. We've all been there. A tragedy or betrayal rocks our foundation, and for a split second all we can do is gasp in disbelief. Leaders have the ability to look at those events and relationships and find the meaning in the situation, creating something useful and developing a positive plan of action.[10]

So what makes a woman in ministry a real leader? "The Bible offers

> Great women leaders aren't just born; they develop by building on the lessons of their times.

many accounts of leaders as prophets, priests, chiefs, and kings. Such leaders served as initiators, symbols, representatives, and examples to be followed. In the Old Testament, Moses led the Hebrews out of Egypt, and Joshua led them to the Promised Land."[11] Their leadership roles were as varied as those of women leaders today.

Many other significant leaders, including Abraham, Esther, Ruth, David, and Solomon, were singled out through detailed stories of their leadership behavior and their relationships with God and their people. God, the ultimate leader of His people, chose those leaders just as He chooses leaders today, to instruct and guide His people and to translate His commands and laws for them.[12]

The New Testament contains leadership lessons for today's leaders in stories about Jesus and His disciples, and His relationship with the groups who gathered to listen to Him.[13] "God created humankind to exist with a purpose of such significance that it gives meaning to life. Regardless of whether one's sphere is humble or quite extensive, God, in His wisdom, understands how it all fits together."[14]

Women leaders have a highly visible role in their organizations, their churches, and their communities. As a result, they face intense pressure to ensure that congregants, customers, and donors are satisfied and engaged. A high level of satisfaction and engagement is essential to encourage followers to contribute constructively to the advancement and improvement of their organization, church, or community.

Effective leadership by women is, therefore, an essential element of building and sustaining significant outcomes for any organizational initiative. Despite the fact that effective leadership is a prominent and important concern, especially for women leaders in a ministry context or women pastors, there is limited empirical research that specifically examines how to build competent and inspirational "transformissional" leadership in this role.

So, what makes a woman leader highly effective? What core skills and traits should she possess? I've learned in my years as a senior pastor and coach that effective women leaders all possess five distinct attributes: (1) missional, (2) reframing, (3) connecting, (4) engaging, and (5) renewing.

Effective women leaders must have the ability to transform their organizations or congregations and infuse basic biblical principles, constructing a framework for stewardship and guidance. Leaders and pastors require high levels of personal artistry to respond to challenges, ambiguity, and paradox. "They need a sense of choice and personal freedom that lets them find new patterns and possibilities in everyday thoughts and deeds. They need the kind of versatility in thinking that fosters flexibility in action."[15] Increasing your abilities in these five attributes will give you that versatility!

ESSENTIAL ATTRIBUTES OF LEADERSHIP

Missional: This is the foundation of inspiration for effective women leaders as it guides their personal lives and propels their professional pursuits by sustaining their optimistic energy. A strong sense of calling offers grit and generates positive purpose to every challenge.

Reframing: A "transformissional" woman leader can change her perspective on how she is experiencing events, ideas, concepts, or emotions to find the most valuable positive alternative for the purpose of moving ahead, adapting, and implementing solutions for achieving goals. Being able to choose to see a different perspective is essential to problem-solving, decision-making, and new learning.

Connecting: By elevating people's thinking about themselves, effective women leaders sustain strong relationships through every part of their lives. By maintaining authentic community, they employ mentoring, collaborative partnerships, and team building as part of a warm holistic sphere of reciprocity that undergirds their continued success.

Engaging: "Transformissional" leaders own the process and the outcomes by maintaining a comprehensive awareness of their team, their strategy, and their plan. With self-clarity, these women leaders have found their voice, and they use it. They take responsibility and get it done.

Renewing: If they are to succeed both professionally and personally, it is critical for effective women leaders to practice spiritual disciplines in the pursuit of personal spiritual formation. Effective women leaders manage their boundaries and their energy to detoxify their bodies, minds, and spirits.

ESSENTIAL ATTRIBUTES FOR
EFFECTIVE WOMEN LEADERS IN MINISTRY

These attributes are the foundation that ensures a relevant and meaningful leadership experience for women who serve God and others while working at the individual, community, and church organizational levels. Simultaneously synthesizing all these variables is a significant challenge. Together, we will explore leadership and the application of leadership for women in a ministry context. I will also offer coaching support to equip and strengthen each woman leader.

COACHING STAGES: IMPROVING INCH BY INCH

Do you remember watching western shows on television when you were a kid, and seeing the stagecoach pulled by a team of horses dashing across the California desert? Masked bandits chased at a full gallop, shooting pistols in the air. Can you see them? The coach driver was perched on top, snapping his whip to encourage the horses to pull harder. The horses ran at full speed to escape the thieves who wanted to rob the precious cargo inside the stagecoach. A hundred and fifty years ago, these coaches were the backbone of commerce and communication across Europe and the United States.

As I envision those stagecoaches full of expectant passengers, I correlate our coaching relationship to that image. Each stagecoach progressed from one stop to the next on a long, difficult journey. The process was uncomfortable and strenuous. It took commitment to travel the distance and not give up when the road was rough or threatening. The horses were conditioned to pull hard in one direction—forward.

You can think of me as your coach. I assure you, we won't go backward. Wherever you find yourself today—right now—this is where we will begin. Yes, you have a story, and it is true. Yesterday happened. But the simple truth is you can't change yesterday. Coaching is about moving forward. So although you may have experienced terrible hardship or been victimized or misunderstood, we must think of yesterday in a simple acronym: TBU—true but useless. Your past may be true. Your perceptions of painful situations in your ministry or personal life may all be absolutely true. Perhaps, as a woman you faced unfair opposition. However, today, we are beginning here and now. Coaching moves in only one direction—*forward*.

I have dedicated three chapters to each leadership attribute. The third chapter of each group provides coaching strategies designed to help you get unstuck. Working together, we'll see you move from where you are to where you want to be. This is about taking intentional action, moving forward, and improving your performance in every area of your life— including your ministry leadership.

Our coaching relationship will be based on an agreement to accept biblical truth. God has an amazing plan for your life, and the Holy Spirit dwelling inside your heart already has the solutions to every obstacle you'll ever face. We're changing your thinking to activate sustained growth in your leadership, and it will impact every area of your life.

I don't offer my personal solutions to your life dilemmas. Instead, you'll answer key questions that will guide you to the positive solution you seek. You see, I believe the answers are already inside you, simply waiting for the right question.

Why ask? "The greatest challenge to any thinker is stating the problem in a way that will allow a solution."[16] Questions have the power to change your perspective, jump-start your creativity, push you to think things through, call you to action, and empower you to believe in yourself. Together, you and I can ask questions and employ tools designed to strengthen your ability to meet each moment in your growing leadership ministry with concrete action.

In the words of Rudyard Kipling, "I keep six honest serving men, they taught me all I knew; their names are What and Why and When, and How and Where and Who." Quite simply, questions cause us to think, create answers we believe in, and motivate us to act on our ideas. Asking moves us beyond a passive acceptance of what others say and eliminates the easy choice of staying stuck in present circumstances. Shifts in our personal world occur because our perception of what we experience changes through the questions we ask. Seeking answers to new questions changes our thought processes so we can function differently and create new experiences.

Jesus said, "Ask and it will be given to you; seek and you will find; knock and the door will be opened to you. For everyone who asks receives; the one who seeks finds; and to the one who knocks, the door will be opened" (Matt. 7:7–8). This is the biblical process of change for every Christian. This asking-knocking-and-seeking effort opens the door of opportunity to us as we step through into new territory. By simply asking, we jump-start our future pathway to open doors.

Our coaching relationship will change your awareness of your surroundings, stimulating you to new actions and changing your world.

Your brain will actually change with the new questions you ask. Coaching helps you see this process from a new perspective and engage in the whole creative process at a higher, more purposeful level. Your questions, the answers, and the resulting actions you take will not only change you, but the world around you.

Coaching moves in only one direction —forward.

I submit that the process of coaching—asking, seeking, knocking—is the most powerful ministry you might ever have. Simply put, by changing you—you change the world. The small personal changes you make absolutely impact others, and focusing on yourself and changing who you are as a person might be the greatest leadership accomplishment of your life. By becoming the person you were designed to be, you could have the biggest impact on the world.

Questions can also redefine relationships. Whenever I'm mentoring, consulting, or advising, I am the expert. At that moment, our relationship is weighted toward me as the one superior in knowledge and/or experience. However, when I move into the coach approach and begin to ask you the questions, then our relationship shifts. I become your peer. My questions honor your ideas and experiences, while they communicate your value. You see, because this asking approach to problem-solving changes the relationship, it also changes you. The flow of ideas between two people stimulates our growth and development. Asking questions and listening for the answers is the key.

As your leadership development coach, here is why I will ask you hard questions:

1. *You already have the answers.* No one knows you like you know yourself. Your experiences and memories are the most valuable asset you have. The expert on your situation is *you*. Plus, as a believer in Jesus, you know the Holy Spirit resides within you. As you pray and work hard to answer each coaching question, your lifetime of memories will kick in with the Spirit's leading, pushing you forward to the answers you seek.

SHATTERING THE STAINED GLASS CEILING

I believe God wants you to thrive in every area of your life. As a Christian leader, I also believe He has already provided every resource you need for your ministry to grow and flourish. Therefore, as your coach, let me assure you that you must have the answers to the questions of your life already buried inside you. As you honestly grapple with the tough questions, you'll ignite your creativity and unleash the Holy Spirit to bring new solutions to the surface of your mind. God has created unlimited resources for you to access, but it will take some purposed commitment from you to dig out your own priceless treasure.

2. *Your answers tie you to your solution.* This leadership development coaching begins with the assumption that <u>the key to making change is becoming motivated to do it.</u> Research shows, and my experience has confirmed over and over, that we're far more motivated to act on our own ideas and solutions rather than on someone else's plans. This means your solution has the greatest potential for results in your life. Asking questions creates buy-in, and your buy-in will get results for you.

    People often ask for coaching when they face a major decision. However, what is interesting to me is that it soon becomes clear more than 90 percent of the time that they already know what to do. By pushing yourself to answer the coaching questions in this book, you'll develop the self-confidence to act on the path God has already placed in your heart.

3. *Your answers shape your future.* <u>Your leadership capacity is only limited by your ability to accept responsibility.</u> Being a leader often means seeing a problem as an opportunity and taking action to bring a solution. Asking "What can I do about that?" moves you away from depending on others for the answers toward taking leadership in the situation. The effort you exert to answer the questions will build your responsibility muscles and, in turn, build your leadership strengths.

FIVE ESSENTIAL LEADERSHIP ATTRIBUTES

THE BENEFITS OF LEADERSHIP COACHING FOR YOUR MINISTRY

> Your greatest energy and highest satisfaction will only be sustained in pursuit of your calling.

Pursue fulfillment in your life by accomplishing your mission. It all begins with meaning. Your leadership in a ministry context is about fulfilling God's mission for your life. Your greatest energy and highest satisfaction will only be sustained in pursuit of your calling. Knowing what it is and how to grow your capacity to lead will occur as you apply systematic development growth strategies. Identifying your vision and integrating it into your everyday life happen as you bring structure to your leadership mindset.

Achieve inner clarity. Often as a woman leader, this is the most difficult element to achieve. More than ever, you have a great diversity of opportunities. You must choose your path or others will choose it for you. You must also redefine your choices as you grow. What is important for you today may be different for you in three, five, or ten years.

Strengthen your personal foundation. Women leaders who seek help from a professional coach want more—sometimes much more. If this is you, then you already realize that you must make specific changes in your personal and professional life to get more of what you desire. These changes are going to take time and effort.

Find your balance. The Bible teaches that you are body, mind, and spirit. Each is interconnected and should be in balance. When one area is out of sync, it affects the others. Through the application of this coaching strategy, you can gain forward traction in your life as a whole: personal relationships, health, spiritual formation, professional growth, self-development, and more. As you focus holistically on your essential leadership attributes, you'll achieve peace of mind, more energy, and a deeper sense of self-fulfillment.

Foster personal accountability. This is a commitment you must make in prayer to God. (1) Ask God to help you engage in the process of leadership development. (2) Next, ask Him to set authority leaders in your life you can trust to submit yourself into an accountability relationship. (3) Share your personal goals and your intention to execute the coaching strategies with this trusted individual. (4) Pray together about your vision for your future, and *then* (5) give this person permission to hold you accountable.

Get an edge in your life and career. Most women leaders operate as though they can do everything without help. To be honest, no one ever accomplishes anything of value without others. Ministry is a team sport, and it requires unity. By opening up to honest evaluation, you are giving the Holy Spirit and your family, friends, and coworkers the opportunity to reveal your blind spots, build your capacity, and energize your drive.

You have made the right, life-changing decision by picking up this coaching strategy. Now, it's time to begin!

THINGS TO CONSIDER:

1. When you hear the phrase "transformissional leadership," what does that mean to you?

   - Leadership that reconciles others to God in some way

2. How are you currently missional in your life and leadership?

   - My job is missional and I am training students to be missional as well

3. When you face a difficult situation, how are you able to reframe it, looking at it from a more positive perspective?

   - Looking at the situation as an opportunity to learn or gain new skills

4. Take a moment to think about the community you have surrounded yourself with: mentors, friends, other leaders, partnerships. Is that the community that will help you move forward? If not, what can you do to build your sense of community?

   Yes it is.

5. Are you engaging in your leadership and life? How do you take responsibility and ensure your voice is heard?

   - Still figuring that out in this new staff/campus

6. How are you currently engaged in personal spiritual formation?

   - Daily QT, reading, consistent time with others who are growing

PART 1

LEADERSHIP ATTRIBUTE: MISSIONAL

We are God's masterpiece. He has created us anew in Christ Jesus,
so we can do the good things he planned for us long ago.

EPHESIANS 2:10, NLT

ATTRIBUTE AFFIRMATION:
AS I ELEVATE MY THINKING—I ELEVATE MY LIFE.[1]

CHAPTER FOUR

YOUR DIVINE DESTINY

There are only two lives we might live: our dream or our destiny.
Sometimes they are one in the same, and sometimes they're not. Often our
dreams are just a path to our destinies.

—GLENNON DOYLE MELTON

Do you know how amazing you are? You are a once-in-all-creation, one-time event. You are new. You are a custom creation made by God. Because you are one-of-a-kind, no one can predict to what heights you might climb. Even you won't know until you step up. You may not be able to see your undeveloped potential, but it's there. The untapped creative abilities inside you are *enormous* no matter your age, your genetic makeup, or your past experiences. Even though you might think of yourself as merely average, you are the latest in a long line of women leader success stories. Your hidden strengths are trying their best to emerge in your ministry. Let them out!

Because you have picked up this book, I know you have moments when you sense much more is possible for you. In those moments, you know you'll regret it if you don't explore the possibilities. Yes, there is greatness in you. I'm certain of it! We don't know specifically what kind of greatness, that's for you to discover and decide for yourself.

Now all you need to do is allow yourself to acknowledge the possibilities ahead. The very act of doing so is the first step in creating the environment where those possibilities, like tiny seeds, will come to life and grow. Think about what you're reading, and as you take steps to put the new ideas into action, you'll add light and water to the already fertile ground of your

> God created you with everything you need to make your calling a reality and to help others develop their calling.

future. You'll start to notice changes, and so will the people around you. You'll begin to feel you are living in harmony with your deepest desires and dreams. Your innermost self will become energized.

God created you with everything you need to make your calling a reality and to help others develop their calling. All you need is a willingness to change and to grow. There's no doubt you'll be successful in this process—you've already begun.

This process doesn't have to be a struggle or a battle. All lasting growth and sustainable change start on the inside and work their way out to become reality. You don't have to overcome or suppress who you are now in order to become a better version of yourself. As you focus on God's purpose for your life, you'll gain the traction to stay on mission. God created your unlimited mind, and He provided you with a unique combination of talents to help you achieve that mission.

You have an amazing mind. Did you know your brain weighs about three pounds and is made up of one hundred billion cells called neurons?[1] That's equivalent to the number of stars in the Milky Way! "The brain is made up of over 100 billion nerve cells with each brain cell connected to around 10,000 other cells, which equals around 1,000 trillion connections in your brain."[2]

Talent is God's gift to you. What you do with your talents is your gift back to God, the people in your world, and people yet unborn! If singing, dancing, math, music, acting, cooking, or speaking publicly come to you easily—then that's your talent! However, a talent is only useful when we have the leadership courage to fulfill its purpose in our lives. If it's easy for you to be a pastor, teacher, a motivational speaker, worship leader, administrator, or fund-raiser—why not be a *great* one?

I'm not exaggerating when I say you are a masterpiece! The Bible says

God created us and has a plan for each of us. Sometimes we wonder what life is all about, but the Bible teaches we are not an accident. Your birth didn't surprise God. Perhaps your parents didn't even want you to be born, but God did. "I am your Creator. You were in my care even before you were born" (Isa. 44:2, CEV). You exist today because God wanted to create you. It isn't fate, chance, luck, or coincidence that you are breathing at this very moment.

I love these words from Pastor Rick Warren: "God prescribed every single detail of your body. He deliberately chose your race, the color of your skin, your hair, and every other feature. He custom-made your body just the way he wanted it. He also determined the natural talents you would possess and the uniqueness of your personality."[3] There once was a day you didn't exist—but there will never be a day when you won't.

"For we are His workmanship [His own master work, a work of art], created in Christ Jesus [reborn from above—spiritually transformed, renewed, ready to be used] for good works, which God prepared [for us] beforehand [taking paths which He set], so that we would walk in them [living the good life which He prearranged and made ready for us]" (Eph. 2:10, AMP).

If you have picked up this book and read this far, you were born to lead!

BORN TO LEAD

Many years ago, a young couple serving as itinerant evangelists in South Florida were expecting their first baby. In one of the evening services, a woman in the audience walked up to the very pregnant mom-to-be and said, "I have a most unusual portable baby crib. It was given to me by my mother because she knew my husband and I would be traveling a great deal. This baby crib is unique because it folds down into a suitcase. The suitcase is perfect for transporting easily. My son has outgrown the crib, and I would like to offer it to you and your husband so you can travel with it when your new baby arrives."

The young mom-to-be said, "I think I would love to have that portable baby crib. I'll use it every day. Thank you so much!" So the woman brought the ingenious suitcase baby crib to the young couple, and after they concluded their series of meetings they took it on the road with them. Their new baby boy was born, and sure enough the suitcase baby crib was a fabulous solution for setting up a portable nursery everywhere they went.

As the months went by and the baby boy came closer to his first birthday, he was so active his parents had a hard time keeping him in the crib. When the young evangelist couple went back to the South Florida area, the new mother wanted to return the crib back to its owner. As she handed it back, she told the woman, "We've loved using that suitcase baby crib so much! It set up and went down so easily. And we particularly loved the zippered netting over the crib so our son could nap outside. We would keep the crib, but our boy is just too big and active. Thank you so much for allowing us to use it!"

As days went by, the lady with the crib and her family moved from South Florida to Kellogg, Idaho, where they settled into a new home and joined a local church. During a series of evangelistic rallies, a fiery young evangelist and his wife were the ministry guests. The young wife was expecting her first child. When the woman with the crib noticed the pregnancy, she went up to the couple and said, "I see that you're expecting a new baby, and I own the most unusual portable baby crib for traveling. It's designed to fold down into a suitcase. My husband and I have traveled extensively with it, but I would like to give it to you to use on the road in your ministry. Would you like to have it?"

The young mother-to-be quickly answered, "Absolutely, yes! I would love to have it! Thank you so much! As we minister on the road, we stay in people's homes all the time. Often there is no nursery and having a portable crib would make all the difference for us. Thank you!" So the young evangelist couple took the suitcase baby crib and used it for their baby daughter.

Thirty-seven years later, my husband, Rich, was preaching in a church in Spokane, Washington. At the end of his message, an elderly woman approached him and said, "Are your parents John and Bonnie Wilkerson?"

My husband nodded and her eyes widened. She quickly went on, "Are you married to Robyn Buntain? Are her parents Lorraine and Fulton Buntain?" My bewildered husband nodded again.

She threw her hands in the air and shook her head in amazement. "This is incredible, impossible; no way can this be true! You see, I loaned my portable baby crib to your mother, Bonnie. She traveled with my crib, and you slept in it until you were almost a year old. Your mom returned it when you outgrew it. When my family moved from South Florida to Idaho we moved the crib with us. In Idaho, we attended a church service where we met Robyn's parents. Robyn's mother, Lorraine, was expecting her, and I gave her parents that same suitcase baby crib so they could use it for her!"

She exclaimed in utter shock, "It's impossible, but Rich, you were the baby who slept in that crib. And as hard as it is for me to believe, the next baby who slept in that crib was your wife, Robyn! Your parents never knew Robyn's parents. You were born in Florida. Robyn was born in Washington. Can you believe God somehow arranged for me to meet your parents, loan them the crib, and then transport it four thousand miles to where I gave it to Robyn's parents? You spent the first year of your life sleeping in that crib, and Robyn spent the first year of her life in that same bed. How could that be a coincidence?"

My husband was speechless. At that point we had already been married seventeen years, and it seemed highly unlikely to him. He called me to ask about the story. It seemed too outrageous to be true, but after talking to both our mothers sure enough it was the case. Rich's mom laughed to remember how rambunctious baby Rich had been. Now she said she knew why she had felt so compelled to return the crib. God must have been leading her to do it.

In fact, my mother told us how she had loved the portable suitcase baby crib so much she had kept it stored in her garage! One of the amazing features of the crib she loved the most was the custom netting that shielded her baby girl so she could set the crib up outdoors for me to nap. Mom noted that because she and Dad quit traveling as evangelists when my first sister was born, she never used the crib again for her other three babies. I was her only baby to use that crib.

Rich was born September 1, 1952, in West Palm Beach, Florida. I was born September 29, 1953, in Seattle, Washington. Our parents didn't know each other. Even though we were born four thousand miles apart, as infants we had both slept in the same borrowed baby crib the first year of our lives!

Today, Rich and I still have the portable suitcase baby crib. I keep it as my faith builder, always proving to me the simple truth: I am not an accident. God knows my name. Coincidence? You think so? For me, it takes more faith *not* to see God's hand in my life. God has a life plan for my husband and me, and for our lives together.

You were born for this! "God doesn't play favorites."[4] The Bible clearly states God has a plan for you. Our steps are ordered even when we are unaware or unable to make choices. God is working on your behalf all the time, with the best intentions for you. I hope our story of the suitcase baby crib sparks faith in you, just as it has strengthened my confidence to look for God's purpose in every situation in my life. As I'm making choices, going through the struggle of day-to-day life, I recall the story of that baby crib and it encourages me to believe that my mission, my marriage, and my ministry are all in God's hands.

Start believing in your own story today. Your birth and the circumstances of your birth were all planned from the start with your highest potential. You chose to pick up this book, and that's evidence that you have leadership in the fabric of who you are.

THE WAY YOU SEE YOUR LIFE SHAPES YOUR LIFE

How do you view God's mission for your life? You may be basing your life on a small, faulty perspective instead of on the big idea God has planned for you. God wants to use you in the mission He created just for you. He has assigned you a life-calling. It's an assignment just for you. The apostle Paul said that David completed the work God set out for him (Acts 13:36). This shows us why God declared that David was "a man after my own heart" (Acts 13:22). David knew his mission, and he fulfilled God's purposes for him by obeying God's call. David was far from perfect, but he persevered in his divine purpose.

What do you want to be written on your gravestone? By fulfilling God's mission in my life, I believe I am preparing for an eternity with Him. According to Romans 14:12, "each of us will give an account of ourselves to God." We will each be given the opportunity to hear God say, "Well done, good and faithful servant" (Matt. 25:23, ESV). This phrase is the ultimate definition of a life lived intentionally, satisfying God's call.

> God is working on your behalf all the time, with the best intentions for you.

You were born at the exact right time, on the exact right day, in the exact right place for your one-of-a-kind mission here on earth. No other time in God's timetable would be more perfect for you than right now. No past or future generations can serve God's purposes for this current generation. Only we can. Like Esther, God created you and me "for such a time as this" (Est. 4:14, ESV). God is looking for women to use. The Bible says, "The eyes of the LORD search the whole earth in order to strengthen those whose hearts are fully committed to him" (2 Chron. 16:9, NLT). Real happiness comes from doing and knowing God is pleased with our lives. "When we discover and unleash our God-given influence, we position ourselves to lead with passion and purpose that defy our personal limitations."[5]

THINGS TO CONSIDER:

1. Take a moment to imagine your future, full of possibilities and wonder. List three of those possibilities here.

   • _Leader or director in XA_
   • _Business owner or teacher of skills overseas_
   • _____

2. Think about the talents God has gifted you with. What do you think your five most valuable talents are?

   • _Administration/Planning_   • _____
   • _Creativity_   • _____
   • _Mentoring/Empathy_

3. How will those talents help you as you grow in your life and leadership?

   I can adapt with creativity and can plan strategically for what comes my way.

4. We all have a story God created just for us. How has your story affected your perceptions of your abilities as a leader?

   Some of my story (high school/WayPoint) makes me encouraged. Other parts (marriage, elementary school, mom) discouraged me.

5. Do you view God's mission for your life as a positive, affirming mission or as an unattainable frustration? What can you do to make your view more positive and active as you begin your journey to success?

   I feel like I keep getting a lot of opportunity to succeed, but often times doubt myself, or fear what others think of me.

CHAPTER FIVE

MISSION MAKES MOMENTUM

"Before I formed you in the womb I knew you, and before you were born I consecrated you; I appointed you a prophet to the nations."

—JEREMIAH 1:5, ESV

Women leaders have a strong sense of mission in every part of their lives. Being an excellent mother requires a commitment to mission. Staying married when our culture gives permission to give up on family solidarity necessitates personal mission. Persevering in your calling to ministry will demand that your mission is crystal clear to you. God blesses us with a universal charge to be on mission in every area of our lives. He created a mission for you to help you flourish and thrive. *Staying on mission is your pathway to find meaning in all your experiences.*

Recently I was driving a busy freeway, going home in the dark from a late-night office appointment. To redeem the time wasted sitting in traffic, I will often get on my cell phone to make calls to friends and family. Visiting and laughing over the phone is the perfect way to offset the stress of rude drivers and lengthy wait times. I got so caught up in my conversation that I didn't notice I had passed my freeway exit toward home. Lights and buildings whirred by when suddenly I realized I was miles and miles north of my little town in the Miami metroplex. I was stunned! Usually, I depend on my phone to guide me through the freeway maze, but since I was mindlessly chatting, the map application had not shouted directions to me. Because I wasn't using my map, but driving ahead in the dark, I found myself declaring out loud, "How did I get here?"

In everyday life, missing a freeway exit is an easy fix since all I had to do was turn around. Once I focused my attention back on my destination, all I needed to do was turn on my cell phone application and go in the right direction. Using the map application in my phone empowered me to stay on course and get home safely—even in the dark.

Staying on mission keeps us energized so we can reach our destination. However, unless we've taken the initiative to stop and clarify for ourselves what our mission is, we can miss out on our greatest source of power. What we need for our life journey is a life application. By reading this book, and pushing yourself through the coaching exercises, you are creating a growing awareness of your personal mission.

Someone has said, "The greatest discovery of my generation is that a human being can alter his life by altering his attitudes. The great use of life is to spend it for something that will outlast it." The only things we know will last forever are the eternal human beings we interact with every day. This thought gives us the perspective to remember that our mission to serve others is the greatest purpose we can accept!

GOD'S MISSION—*MISSIO DEI*

Your mission is directly linked to God's mission. The Bible reveals an overarching meta-story from Genesis to Revelation, showing that God is on a mission to bless humanity, His *missio Dei*. His mission to create a people He could enjoy a relationship with began in the Garden of Eden.[1]

Adam and Eve lived in the garden of Eden and enjoyed a loving, intimate relationship with God. This simple vision of the beginning of human history reminds us that the core purpose underlying God's mission remains the same—God wants to be in a relationship with His people, those created in His image. He wants His people to unite with Him in love, praise, worship, and thanksgiving.[2] And He has called you to help in that mission.

Aristotle spent his adult life trying to figure out why we do what we do. His conclusion? "People reach 'eudaemonia' (a contented state of flourishing) when they are fully using their unique personal talents, thereby fulfilling their function in life."[3] In simpler terms, if you want to thrive, you must use the gifts God gave you fully. No holding back, no second thoughts about every decision.

Knowing your mission, keeping it at the forefront of your life, enables you to push yourself to the edge of your capacity and then farther. Without meaning, work is an endurance test between vacations. Remember Haley, the woman who was stuck? She had lost sight of her mission. With mission comes a sense of meaning that makes any job a calling.

> With mission comes a sense of meaning that makes any job a calling.

Deploying your greatest strengths into the achievement of a meaningful purpose brings the energy you need to break through everyday goals, opening your life to long-lasting, sustainable happiness and satisfaction. There's no doubt mission is a defining attribute among women leaders in ministry. It also helps redefine your priorities when circumstances are out of your control.

FORWARD LIVING: YOUR PASSION IS YOUR POWER

When the phone rang on my office desk, I picked it up to hear my parents who were both on the line. "Hello? Robyn, is that you?" my Dad's voice was husky. A moment of silence, then my mom spoke up, "It's incredible, and I could never dream it would happen, but the brand-new church has burned to the ground!" She took a breath and then went on, "We can't believe the loss. Somehow an electrical fire started in the middle of the night. The entire place went up in flames, and to stop it from spreading to other buildings the fire trucks had to drench everything in water. It's a total loss. Everything is burned except the gymnasium, so we're trying to dig through the mess and set the church up in there." My mom sounded exhausted. We were all in a state of shock. What would happen next?

My parents were pastors of a thriving church in the Pacific Northwest, and they had already worked thirteen years to build the congregation. Only recently, they had moved into a brand-new campus complex including offices, a 1,200 seat auditorium, classrooms, and a new gym. Mother to four children, and the volunteer church office administrator, my mom was always the steady hand on the wheel of our lives. I was already married and living in California, but even through the phone lines I could hear the desperation in her voice.

During the summer of 1965, Mom and Dad had moved our young family of three girls and one boy from Southern California back to mom's hometown of Tacoma, Washington. Making the move north had been a big personal sacrifice for Mom, as she was not interested in returning to her roots and the slow pace of her family's Norwegian immigrant past. Sunshine and shopping malls were a much more interesting lifestyle to the young, enthusiastic clergy couple, but watching the nightly news revealed a dark shift in youth culture erupting with sex, drugs, and rock and roll. My parents saw the coming cultural storm on the horizon and made the less-exciting choice to accept an invitation from the pulpit committee at First Assembly of God in Tacoma.

Now, after more than a decade of work, the fire had destroyed everything. However, had it? Only days before the fire, my parents had received a telephone call with the exciting invitation to return to Southern California to assume a new position to pastor a large congregation. They were praying over the decision to move when the fire changed everything.

Mom recounts standing all bundled up in the cold night air along the fire line, watching the towering fire destroy their hard work and dreams. After the firefighters quenched the flames, as she looked across the mounds of ashes, she realized hundreds of people were also there. When the fire had broken out, news of the emergency had quickly flashed across the community. Entire families and neighborhood activists had run to the burning church. Together, they stood arm in arm, weeping as the blaze encompassed the precious edifice and all its contents.

Rushing into the water, adults and children of all ages began lifting Bibles, books, chairs, musical instruments, choir robes, office supplies, nursery furniture, and thousands of other items out of the mess and moved it all down the hill into the gym. With great intensity, Mom told how she marveled to watch the energy billow bigger and bigger across the crowd as they feverishly worked together to rescue their church. Dad was overwhelmed with waves of emotion, coming to tears as he felt the strength of his congregation's commitment to work in unity for one common purpose: to rebuild.

That surge of purpose and vision galvanized and sharpened my parents' mission. When that fire happened they were already middle-aged, successfully married parents and career professionals. They already knew they were called into ministry. They already knew they were operating in their gifts and their strengths. But going back to the basics of a renewed commitment to their original mission became the compelling force of their lives. Following the fire, on the next Sunday morning they announced to the community newspaper and the congregation, "We will rebuild! However, the new church will be bigger and better than we had before, because we learned where all the improvements could go!"

That mission carried my parent's ministry for another thirty-seven years. They built one of the Northwest's first megachurches—before the word was coined. On that sprawling campus, they also built a 750-student school, and a senior housing and assisted-living center including restaurants and a sports complex. My father and mother continued to work full time as pastors until Dad's eightieth birthday. In his retirement, as pastor emeritus, he continued to go to work every day to serve the church he loved so much. His personal mission to build that church continued to give him boundless energy and enthusiasm until he went to heaven at age eighty-six. My mother continues to live her mission by using every day to see her family and her church continue to thrive. At ninety years old, her mission propels her forward. We must live every minute in purpose and drive!

COACHING TO YOUR MISSION

Your life mission is your GPS for life. Mission is the point of everything. While mission statements seem only recently to have sprung into awareness, they've been around for centuries. Jesus crafted His entire life around His mission statement: "I have come that they may have life, and have it to the full" (John 10:10). Every activity He undertook—whether turning water into wine, playing with children, holding seminars by the sea, or challenging the current religious system—was a result of His mission statement. His mission encompassed His work life, His personal life, and His leisure time.

Your mission statement is a positive prophecy for your future. To grow your leadership, you must identify and pursue your life purpose. By taking the time to define and focus what your life mission is, your strength for living will increase. Daily choices will become easier as you gain clarity and make decisions with confidence. Understanding your life purpose produces a sense of significance and offers direction for how to live a *focused life*.

A defined mission allows you to align your actions with your core values. By raising your personal awareness of your mission, you increase your life satisfaction! This helps reduce overall stress and frustration. You can then focus on what is important, instead of doing what is expected by others or just dealing with what life throws at you.

Knowing your mission will give you the courage to eliminate anything you are tolerating. Once those irritations are gone, you free your energy to pursue important goals in life while increasing your joy on the journey. Your mission will give you the focus you need to identify and overcome internal obstacles. Being stuck often means being bound by nagging fears and self-doubt. Moving ahead in your leadership requires that you leave fears and doubts behind!

Once you have confirmed your mission, you can create your vision statement and map out goals and action plans. Having clarity of God's call will inspire you to greater obedience to the Lord. Confidence in your calling will grow both your intimacy in your relationship with Him and your kingdom impact. When you embrace your life mission, you'll be able to look back over your life and see God's guiding hand. Taking time to articulate your mission will help you discover that your Creator orchestrated life experiences, deposited inborn passions, and planned an individual life mission for *only* you to fulfill.

As you clarify your mission statement, it will bring focus and center to your calling. God's primary purpose is not for you to *do* something for the world. It is for you to *be* who He designed you to become.

Your mission statement is a positive prophecy for your future.

God's will is for you to maximize your kingdom potential and become more like Christ. In God's eyes, your greatest success lies in your obedience to His purpose for you ("To obey is better than sacrifice" 1 Sam. 15:22).

I speak from experience when I tell you that pursuing your life purpose generates sustainable fulfillment and significance. Living a life of purpose is much more than the pursuit of personal happiness. Happiness is a by-product enjoyed by women leaders who are immersed in the pursuit of accomplishing their mission. Along the journey, they experience joy, success, peace of mind, pleasure, and recognition.

Setting aside time to focus on mission will bring you greater energy, satisfaction, and productivity in both your ministry and in your personal life. You can *immediately* create a better future and a better life by synchronizing your daily decisions to match your mission! Passion fuels your energy, which you filter through your experiences in the service of your greater calling. Now is the time to develop the missional attribute in your life through the coaching process.

THINGS TO CONSIDER:

1. Staying on mission is your pathway to find meaning in all your experiences. Think about ways you have let distractions turn you away from your mission. List a few of those distractions that you plan to deal with here.

   • what others think about me • insecurities
   • what the world calls • past hurts
     "success"

2. What are you most passionate about in your life? How does that passion tie into your mission?

   This is part of God's mission for me.

   – Helping others find truth, meaning, and real life
   – Being in a close relationship w/ God & loved ones.

3. Have you defined your mission? If so, what is your mission statement? If not, take a few minutes now to develop a rough draft of a mission statement for your life and ministry.

   To help make this world be more like God's kingdom in relationships, actions, and visually.

4. How is your mission statement going to help you pursue your life?

   It will help me seek God, work hard relationally, and bring out my creative side

5. Have you developed a plan to set aside time to focus on your mission?

   At the end of this quarter, I will take time to brainstorm more.

CHAPTER SIX

COACHING: YOUR GPS FOR LIFE

Christian life isn't a one-person race. It's a relay. You are not alone; you're part of a team assembled by our unstoppable God to achieve His eternal purposes!

—CHRISTINE CAINE

Being missional means you embrace your quest. You see, I believe we all have a unique calling—an innate drive that pushes us to create positive change in the world. When you pursue that calling, your life is filled with passion and meaning. The big question is: How do you reach this stage of supreme fulfillment? Where do you even start searching for your life mission?

COACHING STRATEGY IMPLEMENTATION

1. Start with prayer—invite the Holy Spirit to infuse your thinking with new ideas and vision.
2. Clarify the goal—write your mission statement.
3. Plan an action strategy—determine what resources or tools you need, where you will sit, and when you will start.
4. Define accountability—how will you make yourself accountable to get it done? Who is your accountability partner?
5. Celebrate every victory—once it's completed, what will you do to reward yourself?

PURPOSE

What is that quest for you? Doing something epic? For many people it takes a while to find their quest. Before you work on creating your mission statement, I suggest you start with this heaven-on-earth exercise. The goal is to find your quest. What do you want? How do you get there? Create a vision in your mind of the world you want! As you answer the questions, come from the realm of *possibility*. Don't constrain yourself. When you attain the results of these questions, you are helping all of humanity by fulfilling your mission. Heaven on earth is deeper than vision.

1.   Recall a time when you experienced "heaven on earth." What was happening? Take a few moments to really think about this. You do know; you have that knowing within you.

     ~Rory + Jen pouring into my life
     - Fun + growing in core at WWU

2.   Imagine you have a magic wand. With this wand you can have heaven on earth. What would you do? Focus in on what you need to do to get there.

     - True community/empathy
     - Place of safety & being oneself
     - Teaching others empathy & self sacrifice.
     - Finding joy in creating

3.   What simple, concrete steps will you take in the next twenty-four hours to have more of that heaven-on-earth experience become real for you?[1]

     - Invite others into relationship
     - Be real about who I am, not faking perfection.
     - Resting + allowing others to rest.

MISSION TO VISION

Laurie Beth Jones described a mission statement this way: "A good mission statement is so easily communicated and understood that a twelve-year-old could understand and repeat it."[2] Developing a mission statement will lead you to participate in self-discovery, training you to be more effective in developing your leadership skills. By doing the hard work, digging deep, you will actively engage coaching concepts for your own growth, including creating your unique mission and vision statements. Discovering your mission is priority as you prepare to develop your leadership capacity. To become the leader God has called you to be, you must make the difficult decision to carve out adequate time to map the road ahead.

Greatness in the kingdom of heaven isn't about doing more than someone else; it's about making the most of what you've been given. Before beginning this coaching exercise, find a private place for yourself. Be ready to write out your thoughts so you can revisit your impressions and revelations. Bring along your Bible, settle yourself in a comfortable position, and allow lots of time to move through the questions.

Don't rush! This is about thinking, praying, and then listening to hear the answers. Pray first, and ask God to help you see your world and yourself in a new way. Read the questions out loud, then write your answers as clearly as possible, conveying your best self. These are contemplative questions, designed to stimulate your thinking. This self-inventory should take several sessions to compose your responses completely.

Your mission statement is a short, written document. It should be easy for you to state quickly in three to five sentences. But you also need to write an expanded explanation of about three to five pages, about one thousand words, to fully describe how your mission applies to the rest of your life.

This is written for your private purposes. You can't hire someone to write it. It must flow from your heart. Start by answering this question: "How do you want to be remembered?" When you are gone, you will leave behind a legacy of memories you created in the lives of those you touched and loved. The purpose of writing your mission statement is to understand that you can be intentional now about what you are doing and why you are doing it.

DESTINY DISCOVERY

1. What do you already know about what you were created to do here on earth?
2. When you were a girl, what did you want to be when you grew up?
3. Where have you already found meaning and purpose in your life?

4. Since every experience in your life can be used to equip you to perform your life purpose, what has your whole life been preparing you to do next?
5. What have you already done that has brought the most value to other people's lives?
6. How has God revealed your life purpose to you?
7. What are you most effective at in your ministry? Where do you have the most impact?
8. Can you identify a sense of purpose that runs through your family history?
9. What is your family's historical legacy of mission and how can you/ why don't you want to be a part of that?
10. What do your family and closest friends say are your greatest strengths and weaknesses? How does this design point toward your life purpose?
11. Imagine looking back over your life. What personal dream would cause you deep regret if you didn't take the risk to fulfill it?
12. If you knew you could change one thing in the world by investing your life to make it happen, what would that be?

DEFINE YOUR OWN SUCCESS

Take a few moments to write a paragraph defining what success means for you.

Personal Mission Statement Assignment: There's no specific format for writing your personal mission statement. Only you will know how to write it, but try to keep it clear, brief, and exciting. Just ask yourself, "What is my calling, my life's aim? What inspires me the most? What activities or services are my core values urging me to pursue?"

What do you see? Your mission is only seen by you. What are you seeing in your life?

What do you see? Some people see an old woman, some people see a young woman. Differences in your perception can change what success looks like to you.

(Image created by W. E. Hill, who published it in 1915 in *Puck* humor magazine.)

WHEEL-OF-LIFE EXERCISE

How satisfied are you with different parts of your life? Circle a number from 1 to 10 next to each of the following areas of life. If you give an item a 1, you are completely dissatisfied with that part of your life. A 10 means you are completely satisfied and couldn't be happier with this part of life. Your overall satisfaction will change from day to day, but try to give an overall assessment of *where you are at present*. Skip any items that don't apply to you.

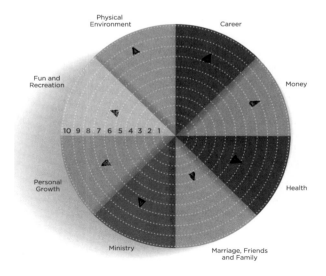

DISSATISFIED/SATISFIED

PHYSICAL HEALTH

1   2   3   4   5   <u>6</u>   7   8   9   10

MENTAL/EMOTIONAL HEALTH

1   2   3   4   5   <u>6</u>   7   8   9   10

CAREER/EMPLOYMENT SATISFACTION

1   2   3   4   5   6   7   <u>8</u>   9   10

FINANCIAL STABILITY

1   2   3   4   5   6   7   <u>8</u>   9   10

MARRIAGE/ROMANTIC RELATIONSHIPS

1   2   3   4   5   <u>6</u>   7   8   9   10

HOME LIFE (IMMEDIATE FAMILY)

1   2   <u>3</u>   4   5   6   7   8   9   10

EXTENDED FAMILY (RELATIVES, IN-LAWS)

1   2   <u>3</u>   4   5   6   7   8   9   10

FRIENDS/SOCIAL LIFE

1   2   3   4   <u>5</u>   6   7   8   9   10

RECREATION/RELAXATION

1   2   3   4   5   <u>6</u>   7   8   9   10

LIFESTYLE (DEGREE OF BUSYNESS)

1   2   3   4   5   <u>6</u>   7   8   9   10

PERSONAL LIFE FULFILLMENT

1   2   3   4   5   6   <u>7</u>   8   9   10

PERSONAL SPIRITUAL LIFE

1 2 3 4 <u>5</u> 6 7 8 9 1 0

CHURCH/SPIRITUAL LIFE

1 2 3 4 <u>5</u> 6 7 8 9 1 0

CURRENT MINISTRY

1 2 3 4 5 6 <u>7</u> 8 9 1 0

PHYSICAL COMFORT (HOUSING, LOCATION, CAR, ETC.)

1 2 3 4 5 6 7 8 <u>9</u> 1 0

Now transfer the scores on the circle chart and connect the points together with a line, making a circular graph. When this is completed, please complete the form again, only this time put a square around the number that indicates *where you would like to be* if things could be ideal! Once again, put the squares on the circle and join them together. What areas have the largest gaps between where you are at present and where you would like to be? These may be areas where coaching can be beneficial.

If you rated an area extremely low, you can see where your forward movement in life is already impaired, like a tire with a nail in it. No matter how strong the tire is, it will go flat in the place where the air (energy) is pouring out. The tire needs to be inflated all the way around to get forward traction. This is true in your life as well.

The life areas you are evaluating in this exercise are:

Body: What you do to take care of yourself—including vacations, personal appearance, grooming, physical health, fitness level, etc.
Mind: Stress levels, mental fitness, sufficient rest
Finances: Income, asset management, retirement
Personal growth: Things you are doing to improve yourself
Environment: Setting, your home, your office, car

Community: Friends, social life, community engagement
Work: Professional life, career, volunteer
Spirit: Spiritual growth, personal-satisfaction levels, happiness
Family: Marriage, children, extended family
God: Your God awareness, Bible study, worship, praise

POSITIVE POWER PRAYER:
COACHING FROM THE INSIDE OUT

God's mission for you is already at work, but to increase your awareness of the Holy Spirit in your life it's important that you base your intention on God's Word. Focused attention is very much like a muscle you can strengthen through exercise. Begin with a prayer of thanksgiving. Be grateful for where you are in your life today. Then, out loud, read one Scripture and insert your first name into the sentence.

As you say the Scripture, declare the promise and envision your mission being activated with every word. Stop. Then, do it again with another Scripture. Pray the Scripture promises and allow them to build hope and faith into your personal mission. Your *mission statement* is your positive prophecy to your future.

- "For I know the plans I have for you [_____], declares the LORD, plans for welfare and not for evil, to give you a future and a hope. Then you will call upon me and come and pray to me, and I will hear you [_____]. You will seek me and find me, when you seek me with all your heart." (Jer. 29:11–13, ESV)
- But you [_____] are a chosen group of people. You are the King's religious leaders. You are a holy nation. You belong to God. He has done this for you so you can tell others how God has called you out of darkness into His great light. (1 Peter 2:9, NLV)
- For we [_____] are God's masterpiece. He has created us anew in Christ Jesus, so we can do the good things he planned for us long ago. (Eph. 2:10, NLT)

- For you formed my inward parts; you knitted me together in my mother's womb. I praise you, for I [_____] am fearfully and wonderfully made. Wonderful are your works; my soul knows it very well. (Ps. 139:13–14, ESV)
- "And I will make of you [_____] a great nation, and I will bless you and make your name great, so that you [_____] will be a blessing." (Gen. 12:2, ESV)
- For He delivered us [_____] and saved us [_____] and called us [_____] with a holy calling [a calling that leads to a consecrated life—a life set apart—a life of purpose], not because of our works [or because of any personal merit—we could do nothing to earn this], but because of His own purpose and grace [His amazing, undeserved favor] which was granted to us in Christ Jesus before the world began. (2 Tim. 1:9, AMP)
- "But I consider my life as worth nothing to myself, in order to finish my mission and the ministry that I [_____] received from the Lord Jesus, to testify to the gospel of the grace of God." (Acts 20:24, LEB)
- "But rise [_____] and stand upon your feet, for I have appeared to you for this purpose, to appoint you as a servant and witness to the things in which you have seen me and to those in which I will appear to you." (Acts 26:16, ESV)
- So God created . . . [_____] in his own image, in the image of God he created [her]. (Gen. 1:27, ESV)
- I [_____] run straight toward the goal to win the prize that God's heavenly call offers in Christ Jesus. (Phil. 3:14, GW)
- I [_____] thank Christ Jesus our Lord, who has granted me [the needed] strength and made me able for this, because He considered me faithful and trustworthy, putting me into service [for this ministry]. (1 Tim. 1:12, AMP)
- "But for this purpose I have caused you [_____] to stand: to show you my strength, and so that my name may be declared in all the earth." (Ex. 9:16, NET)
- For God is at work within you [_____], helping you

want to obey him, and then helping you do what he wants. (Phil 2:13, TLB)

- Just as each one of you [_____] has received a special gift [a spiritual talent, an ability graciously given by God], employ it in serving one another as [is appropriate for] good stewards of God's multi-faceted grace [faithfully using the diverse, varied gifts and abilities granted to Christians by God's unmerited favor]. Whoever speaks [to the congregation], is to do so as one who speaks the oracles (utterances, the very words) of God. Whoever serves [the congregation] is to do so as one who serves by the strength which God [abundantly] supplies, so that in all things God may be glorified [honored and magnified] through Jesus Christ, to whom belongs the glory and dominion forever and ever. Amen. (1 Peter 4:10–11, AMP)

PART 2

LEADERSHIP ATTRIBUTE: REFRAMING

The will of God is never exactly what you expect it to be.
It may seem to be much worse, but in the end it's going to be
a lot better and a lot bigger.

—ELISABETH ELLIOT

ATTRIBUTE AFFIRMATION:
AS I TURN MY THINKING AROUND, I BREAK FREE IN
A NEW DIRECTION TOWARD THE SOLUTION.

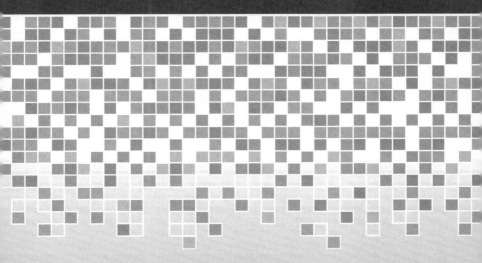

CHAPTER SEVEN

HAVE YOU LOST YOUR MIND?

She lives with a profound confidence that he holds the whole
world (including her) in his hands.

—CAROLYN CUSTIS JAMES

"Rich, have you lost your mind? You can't be serious! Our whole life is
here! You want to uproot our boys from our private school at church and
move us all to the inner city of Miami, Florida? Jonfulton is going to be a
senior in high school, and Richie loves his friends. Graham is in his LIFE[1]
special-needs program that we created for him! Taylor is only eight years
old, but he doesn't want to leave his cousins and grandparents! We live
right next door to my parents; it will be a heartbreak for them to have the
boys move four thousand miles away! Plus, *I don't want to go!* I don't know
anything about urban ministry! Look at me! I'm a Nordstrom-shopping,
middle-aged, white, suburban, soccer mom. I wouldn't fit in!"

I was talking very loud and very fast.

"I was born and raised in the Pacific Northwest. I don't like Florida. I hate
humidity. I can't breathe when it gets hot in Miami. Plus, I'm so different
from the women at that church! Don't even consider it. I'm not going!"

Through prayer, Rich had received a strong direction to shift his
ministry, and he wanted me to support his new plans. At that point, we
had been married twenty-five years, had four sons, owned our home, lived
close to my extended family, and were part of a large church community
in a small town. It was my entire world.

For eighteen years, as an itinerant evangelist, my forty-five-year-old
husband had been traveling across the United States and around the

world. It was his full-time profession. We had worked so hard to transition from being youth pastors ministering in a local church to televangelists. We grew a missions agency to expand his ministry. We had large offices, a big staff, a television ministry, and a full calendar of commitments. Rich was seeking a fresh new identity, and he intended for me to help him make it happen. So here we were having another repetitive argument about Miami. He was tired. He needed a change.

"Okay. I'll go with you to meet with the deacon board, but I don't see the purpose. We are just wasting their time." I finally gave in. Rich ran to the phone to set the travel arrangements from Tacoma to Miami.

We arrived at the Miami airport, and it was exactly as I had remembered. It was the busy, immense, cosmopolitan, international crossroads of the entire Latin world. Non-English conversations were everywhere. No one looked like me. No one talked like me. I was the minority. I hated it!

From the airport, we rushed to the hotel to get ready for the church board meeting that night. Our hosts took us to an authentic Cuban dinner, and then we arrived at the church, only to discover the deacons had been waiting for more than two hours. Needless to say, they were exasperated with us.

Located in the "hood," the place was beyond run-down. The entire church campus was a mess. We faced chipped paint, dilapidated buildings, carpet so worn the color was gone, and a meeting table infested with termites. Rusty folding chairs and a ceiling light fixture missing bulbs set the atmosphere for me. There was no way I was bringing my family and coming to pastor this church.

The meeting progressed as Rich described our vision for the positive possibilities for Trinity Church. Looking back, I believe most of the people present were probably amused to listen to our grandiose picture for their struggling congregation in a highly challenged zip code. Every American urban problem surrounded the church location: gangs, poverty, drugs, violence, broken families, poor schools, crime, racism, and a depressed economic community.

I only saw lack. My husband saw opportunity!

The church invited us to come, and we accepted. So on July 24, 1998, we moved to Miami along with four sons and a dog. Loaded to full capacity, two semitrucks transported us from our existence as a predictable suburban family to super-stressed, urban missionaries. We were the only white family in every way. Our kids were miserable. Extreme culture shock took a heavy toll, but we persevered.

Hungry, homeless people met me every morning in the church parking lot. I actually had to step over them to get into my office. Everywhere I turned, people were desperate, looking for help. Congregants streamed to the office asking for money or jobs. Rich kept on preaching.

Within our first year of pastoring, domestic violence, gang warfare, and murder hit our little flock, resulting in funerals and heartbreak. Trying to navigate the diverse cultures and languages of our community was overwhelming. After a year of attempting to manage this tiny urban church with the same strategies I had experienced all my life in the suburban context of pastoring, I was at my wit's end. I thought that giving up and going back home seemed like the only option. However, my husband and I had made a firm decision together; there was no turning back. God had sent us on a mission, and we had burned the bridges. We had come to build our vision for a megachurch in Miami, and it wasn't going well.

All our money was gone. All our plans and resources were exhausted. In my total frustration one afternoon, I walked outside my office and just gazed around our concrete campus of dilapidated church buildings. It must have been over 100 degrees. I was exhausted. Standing on our cracked, asphalt parking lot, I yelled up at heaven, "Father, can You see me? Did You forget we are here trying to bring healing to this broken community? Can't You send us help?" In a split second, the Holy Spirit answered me, "Robyn are you asking for help to make things look like you? Do you want Me to help you recreate your idea, or do you want Me to help you build *My* church?"

Boom! Suddenly God gave me a brand-new idea. By changing my focus from a church that looked like every church I had ever attended, He opened my vision to a different idea. Instead of seeing the homeless, dirty, smelly, hard-to-serve individuals living under our staircases as vagrants, I asked God to help me see them as He did. Immediately He turned my thinking

> I could relax in knowing that God was going to help us build *His* church. It was only going to happen *His way.* Not mine.

inside out.[2] Hours earlier I had seen these folks as obstacles to my vision; now I had given up my plan. Our mission was the same, but my way of getting the job done had to change. I could relax in knowing that God was going to help us build *His* church. It was only going to happen *His way.* Not mine.

Months passed until one day I came across a tiny advertisement in a Miami newspaper soliciting community agencies to compete for funding to offer summer day camps. We applied, and we won enough money to put on a day camp for five hundred children. It was an amazing success for the church and the community. Through this first partnership alliance, we continued to build partnerships with nonprofit agencies, corporations, banks, schools, universities, businesses, hospitals, and government agencies—federal, state, county, and city. Today we maintain more than 150 partnerships, and we've acquired more than forty million dollars in funding for social services for our community.

You see, our access to "poor people" was our treasure. The "problem" that initially repelled me was the very thing God wanted to use to bless me. Until I was willing to thank Him for the thing I was asking Him to remove, He wasn't able to provide the solution for our family's successful future. It was bigger than just me.

Our church has thrived. Our children have flourished. Jobs have been created. A school has been birthed. The neighborhood has been elevated. Thousands have found Christ and continue to worship with our family a generation later.

By *reframing* my thinking about the situation, I was able to break free toward a solution for community engagement and resources. God promises to help us, but He doesn't promise to help us in the way we choose. He offers His help in the way He chooses. God's ways aren't our ways. To find the answers to the obstacles you are facing in your ministry, are you willing to change your thinking and turn your mind-set inside out? What situation in your life could benefit from forward movement if you were willing to open your mind?

HOW REFRAMING WORKS

When we shift our thinking or our perspective on something, we refer to that new point of view as a "frame." Different frames represent varying possibilities for perceiving the same thing in different ways. When we use frames, they help us interpret the world around us and represent that world to others.[3] Understanding reframing can also give us insight into understanding self-fulfilling prophecies.

Our beliefs unconsciously direct us in our moment-by-moment choices and actions. What we believe actually drives our viewpoint and our mind-set in every situation. Self-fulfilling prophecies have been called the "Pygmalion effect," a term derived from a play that later became the Broadway musical *My Fair Lady*.[4] In the story, Professor Henry Higgins won a bet to prove his opinion that nurture was more powerful than nature. To make his case, he located a crude, unrefined young woman named Eliza Doolittle. With his coaching, she transformed from a street urchin to a charming, enchanting beauty. The fictional story presents how our self-perception, or who we think we are, is a prime basis for how we will experience life. We behave according to who we believe we should be.

Not only does what we believe about ourselves impact our destiny, what we believe about others affects their behavior, even without their knowledge. To demonstrate the *power of belief*, research has shown that a teacher's expectations about her student's future abilities can influence how that student performs in the classroom.[5] Since 1964, Harvard University's Dr. Robert Rosenthal has researched the role of self-fulfilling prophecy in everyday life. His idea was to discover the impact on children's learning scores if teachers were told certain kids were future high achievers.

Rosenthal took a standard intelligence test and renamed it the "Harvard Test of Inflected Acquisition."[6] He then told the teachers it was a new test

What is a disastrous problem for someone else can be an exciting growth prospect for you!

that would predict which children were going to experience a dramatic improvement in their intelligence quotient (IQ) scores. After he gave the test to the kids, without any regard to the actual scores, he randomly selected children's names and reported them as the future high achievers.

Over the next two years, Rosenthal documented that the teacher's expectations really did affect the students. He discovered that those students he reported to the teachers as showing intellectual superiority actually did *increase* their performance—dramatically. The teacher's belief about the potential of the student created an environment where the student did achieve. "What you expect is what you get. We are all familiar with the idea of self-fulfilling prophecy. One way of describing this concept is to say that if we expect something to happen in a certain way, our expectation will tend to make it so."[7]

ALL THINGS ARE POSSIBLE IF WE BELIEVE

Our beliefs shape our perceptions; our perceptions define our experience. We find meaning in our lives from our experiences. This means that when you reframe a situation, you expand your perceptions by offering a new viewpoint through which to see your life circumstances.[8] How my husband saw our inner-city Miami church was exactly the opposite of what I perceived. Here is your leadership principle: What is a disastrous problem for someone else can be an exciting growth prospect for *you!*

Meaning is found inside reframing no matter how bad the circumstances might be. Dr. Victor Frankl, an Austrian neurologist and psychiatrist who survived the Holocaust, wrote *Man's Search for Meaning* in which he described his experiences as a Nazi concentration camp inmate.[9] Inside the horror of that death camp, he chose to envision his future after the war would be over. He kept himself alive by clinging to a vision of how he would enjoy his post-war success. As he clung to his goals, he watched other prisoners die because they couldn't reframe their current situation into a positive future outcome. This led him to articulate the power of finding meaning in all forms of existence, even the brutal ones. Frankl asserted that the way a prisoner imagined his future affected his longevity. Positive envisioning of a purpose gave the prisoner hope. That hope gave life. Frankl believed, "that man's main concern is not to gain pleasure or to avoid pain but rather to see a meaning in his life."[10]

YOU WORK TOO HARD

"You know you work too hard, and it's time to try something new around here. Won't you please pray about this change and help me develop a new leader for the school?" The fifty-year-old, bespectacled male pastor begged earnestly as he hovered over Beth's desk. He was back for the third time to

What you believe shapes who you are. Who you believe you are impacts everything you do.

drop the hint that he wanted to move her out. She had served as the principal for more than three decades, and in recent years the school board had reduced her administrative staff. Now she had no secretary, no vice principal, no counselor, and her boss had finally come out with it. "You can have a new job and not have to work so hard to keep this place going anymore. What do you say?"

He was right. She had worked too hard for the last several years. The school enrollment had dropped, but the budget had been adjusted and the school was in the black. Yes, finding new families to pay the rising tuition, while dealing with discipline, parents, and fund-raising all at the same time was exhausting. It was true. She wasn't getting any younger. After thirty-five years as principal, she was confident she brought great value to the school with her experience and her network of professionals, parents, and pastors. Her husband had died suddenly eight years earlier, and although she had a retirement nest egg, it wasn't enough to live on. Besides—she wasn't actually old! Being sixty-six years old had sounded ancient when she was forty; but now, still feeling healthy and strong, she was just as committed to her calling as she had ever been!

How was she supposed to just retire and quit? It's a new frontier for aging ministry leaders as they attempt to shift from one role to the next new ministry.

Beth made the shift. With courage, she packed up her main office to move into new digs down the hall to become the admissions director. Faith sustained her as she reframed her vision for her mission to move her focus away from student engagement and into fun- raising and development. As a single woman, she began to realize her availability to travel, speak, and create relationships for the school with donors and community partners. Beth recounted her feelings when she phoned to say, "You know, as hard as it was to let go of being the principal, I'm excited to reinvent myself on behalf of building the future for the school. Endowments, scholarships, and strategic planning are exciting to me as I leverage all my experience and relationships to enrich the school for greater effectiveness. Honestly, I feel renewed through prayer, meditation, and waiting on God to inspire me emotionally and physically to have the energy to move forward. Praise the Lord for new ministry leadership opportunities even for this old lady!" What you *believe* shapes who you are. Who you believe you *are* impacts everything you do.

THANK GOD FOR THE FLEAS

Cornelia "Corrie" ten Boom was a Dutch watchmaker and Christian who, along with her father and other family members, helped many Jews escape the Nazi Holocaust during World War II. She was imprisoned for her actions in a Nazi women's labor camp along with her sister Betsie. Corrie wrote years later of her conversation with God regarding the condition of their barracks.

The circumstances for the inmates were unimaginable everywhere in the labor camp, but Corrie had come to discover that her barracks were the most uninhabitable due to an infestation of fleas. According to Corrie, she was complaining to God regarding the fleas when she suddenly realized the fleas kept the prison guards from entering their barracks. *Because* of the fleas, she and Betsie were allowed to lead worship services after the hard days at work, using a Bible they had managed to smuggle in. The very thing she despised was the thing protecting her ministry.[11]

By *reframing* problems, you can get closer to the new ideas, solutions, strategies, and resources you need for a breakthrough in your ministry. To reframe your thinking is to intentionally create a new, positive pathway forward to success. Reframing is an essential attribute if you want to maximize your leadership.

Reframing lets you change your perspective on how you choose to experience relationships, events, ideas, concepts, or emotions to find a more positive alternative for your purpose of moving ahead, adapting, and implementing solutions. Your choice to see a different perspective is essential to problem-solving, decision making, and new learning. "Optimistic thinking is a resilience skill that helps people overcome adversity and reach life goals."[12] Reframing is looking at a situation from a positive frame of mind, and it actually transforms the way you think.

THINGS TO CONSIDER:

1. How has God moved you out of your comfort zone in the past (or right now)?

    - from shy to outgoing   - being a leader
    - public speaking
    - trying new, adventurous things.

2. To find the answers to the obstacles you are facing in your ministry, are you willing to change your thinking and turn your mind-set inside out?

3. What situation in your life could benefit from forward movement if you were willing to open your mind?

    - helping students become more socially adept / mature.

4. What you believe shapes who you are. What false/negative beliefs in your life are currently holding you back?

    - I believe I am less than others in many ways (looks, talents, emotional capacity, friendship, etc.)

5. Take a moment to think about one situation in your life that didn't go the way you wanted. Does your perspective of the situation change when you reframe the circumstances of the situation?

    - UCF
    - I could have viewed it more w/ "what good possibilities are here," rather than being discouraged.

CHAPTER EIGHT

THE POWER OF YOUR POSITIVE PERSPECTIVE

Commit your works to the LORD [submit and trust them to Him], and your plan will succeed [if you respond to His will and guidance].

—PROVERBS 16:3, AMP

Thoughts are things, and they become your reality. If you want to change your life, you first have to change your reality. We each have the ability to choose our thoughts and think things on purpose. In other words, you *don't* have to think about whatever falls into your mind. This is a life-changing revelation! As Proverbs 23:7 (AMP) says, "As [a person] thinks in his heart, so is he." We say it like this: Where the mind goes, your life will follow.

"The thoughts and processes you hold close become your reality."

God is concerned about the hidden heart of the human, the inner life, what we think about. As the Scripture says, the way we think determines how we live and who we are. That's why we need to think about what we're thinking about. It's important for us to understand this. If we don't learn how to take every thought captive to the obedience of Christ (see 2 Corinthians 10:4–5), we won't live the life Jesus died to give us. Christ offers a life of peace with God, peace with ourselves, great relationships, real joy, and the ability to become all God created us to be. It comes down to choosing to believe what God says (the truth) more than we believe our feelings, what other people say, or our circumstances.

"That's a terrible idea. She can't be the executive pastor! First, she's the former pastor's daughter, and second, she has no experience. Who would ever put that young woman in charge of our finances and employees? Having a woman as the leader is a big step for our community. I am not for this idea at all!" He was making his point by tapping the conference table with his fist. As the middle-aged deacon exhaled with dramatic exasperation, he rolled his eyes and looked around the boardroom to assess who was agreeing with his negative opinion.

An older male deacon leaned forward and cleared his throat. "Well, I disagree with you. Sue has lots of valuable experience because she has worked here since she was fifteen years old. She has raised a family and been a pastor's wife for twenty-five years right here in our church. Plus, she has a business degree and has led the finance department for the last ten years. To be honest, no one cares about the legacy of this church more than Sue. She and her family have given their lives to build this work, and she has a lifetime of experience and relationships that she can leverage to help lead the future for the next generation of this ministry! I strongly support her moving into the role—officially—as the new executive pastor. She needs all of us to give our 100 percent support and appreciation!"

It was a new season at this one-hundred-year old church. The board of directors had lots of opinions now that the former pastor had moved into retirement. He had led the church into prominence with his fifty years of continuous leadership, but with his departure it was open season for every church leader to weigh in with their agenda.

"Why do we have to call her a 'pastor'? Why can't she just be a business administrator, or a manager? When we call her a pastor, it makes me feel weird. I don't want to hear a woman preacher that's for sure! Is she going to perform weddings or funerals? I mean I'm just not ready for that!" lamented another elderly male deacon.

The new lead pastor was quiet as he listened to the crossfire of conversation. How could this be the focus of what the church leaders were actually thinking? He couldn't believe his ears. Just because she was a woman, the deacons wanted to disqualify the best leader he had on his team? He firmly believed in her and would fight to convince the deacon board. He knew Sue would succeed because she believed in herself and her call. Her positive attitude and leadership had already benefited the church and would benefit her in this new position.

Women are moving forward in leadership in every part of life. Research echoes what has been found in professional and business contexts, that although there is still much to be gained, women are stepping into ministry in record-breaking numbers.[1] Women are gaining ground.[2] Leadership for women is showing a shift in gender leadership opportunities.[3] As women embrace their leadership calling, there is more opportunity than ever before to lead with a powerful confidence to see positive changes in families, churches, organizations, and communities.

The Bible talks about three actions we must take to acquire a mind that comes to an agreement with God.

1. *"Set your mind and keep focused habitually on the things above [the heavenly things]"* (Col. 3:2, AMP). This is the key to resisting temptation. Before we get into a situation where we'll need to make a choice, we must decide in advance where our intention is focused. By deciding what we will and won't do before temptation shows up, we lay a foundation to make right choices, and we increase our chances to overcome the temptation successfully. For instance, before you get into social situations, decide, "I'm not going to gossip. I'm not going to ruin someone's reputation and offend the Holy Spirit." Other temptations may require you to decide things like, "I'm not going to use language that is toxic today." Or "I'm not going to waste time on selfish arguments." Alternatively, "I'm not going to hang out with people who are bad influences." In other words, we don't need to get ambushed by temptation.

2. *"Do not be conformed to this world . . . but be transformed and progressively changed [as you mature spiritually] by the renewing of your mind"* (Romans 12:2, AMP). Renewing the mind is a constant process. We must take time every day to study God's Word so we

can intentionally think according to what it says. No one is perfect with this, but we need to make progress so we can keep our minds renewed and can grow in our relationship with God.

3. *"Gird up the loins of your mind"* (1 Peter 1:13, NKJV). This is old-fashioned terminology, and you might be wondering what the writer meant. He was saying that we need to get all the trash out of our minds so we can keep "running our race" in Christ Jesus. God intends for you to win the race you are running for Him, as the first-place winner! By clearing out our minds, we are ready for action to follow God's plan for our lives.

One practical way we can accomplish these action steps from God's Word is to have a daily think session. At the end of each part of this book, there are Scriptures and coaching exercises for you to complete. You've already finished the first one. Just sit down and say, "I'm going to think about some things on purpose." Then spend time thinking about Scriptures that renew your mind with the truth about what God says—about His love for you and His plan for you. Insert your name into the coaching Scriptures and envision yourself winning your race. I want to encourage you to write some of the verses down and put them in places where you'll see them every day, like on the bathroom mirror or refrigerator.

Commit to set your mind on God's Word, renewing your mind with truth and getting "stinkin' thinkin'" out of your way. Yes, it might take a little time, but as you continue forward you'll start to enjoy the life God is offering you today. All it takes is a little more progress, one day at a time. The first step to understanding how to control your thoughts is to learn how your brain functions.

BRAIN SCIENCE BREAKTHROUGHS

Coaching works.[4] Applying coaching to your leadership development is a highly effective approach to reaching your goals. Research proves that "coaching has significant positive effects on performance and skills, well-being, coping, work attitudes, and goal-directed self-regulation."[5] Understanding how the brain works can help coaching become your pathway to building sustainable higher capacity in every area of your life.

Quantum physics has proven that the observation process itself changes the properties of the atoms being studied. Since our brains contain billions of neurons made of subatomic components, it makes sense that this principle would also hold true for human particles. In other words, the act of coaching, or observing your thinking, your calling, and your internal self-talk, will have a profound effect on your development.

Thinking is actually a complex chemical process inside the cells of your brain called neurons. The neurons transmit information by firing electrical impulses through synapses. As you learn to think in new ways the connections between the neurons become stronger and the synapses are reinforced.[6] "Cells that fire together, wire together."[7]

Each thought, or firing of the synapses, shapes the connections, a process known as "synaptic plasticity." So your synapses actually strengthen or weaken over time depending on whether you are actively thinking or not.[8] Your changing thoughts, experiences, and feelings are all forming your mind!

This means your every thought is an electrochemical reaction. Each thought stimulates chemicals in magnificently complex electromagnetic waves that would sound like the most exquisite symphony if you could hear them.[9] The brain, the magnificent control center God created, is said to be the most complex organic structure in the universe.[10]

"One of the key practical lessons of modern neuroscience is that the power to direct our attention has within it the power to shape our brain's firing patterns, as well as the power to shape the architecture of the brain itself."[11] Our thoughts are creating our minds, our bodies, and our well being. The good news is we can train our brains to think new and different thoughts!

For centuries philosophers and scientists have questioned how the mind and the brain relate to one another. We are just beginning to understand the essential nature of the bond between body, mind, and spirit. This means brain science supports Scripture.

Research today is confirming what Scripture has taught for thousands of years: "For as he thinks in his heart, so is he" (Prov. 23:7, AMP). Your thinking will determine the outcomes of your life. You can choose to think thoughts that are emotionally destructive and energy depleting, or you can elevate your life by choosing healing positive thoughts. Happier, healthier, wealthier people control their every thought to leverage their energy and to accomplish their life-calling by leading with every resource God has provided.[12]

YOUR ADVANTAGE: A HAPPINESS MIND-SET

Happiness leads to success in every area of your life—work, health, relationships, creativity, and energy. This isn't just something I know. Positive psychology researchers did a meta analysis (a study of other research) of more than two hundred studies of 275,000 people worldwide with amazing results.[13] Happy people tend to be more helpful, creative, prosocial, charitable, altruistic, and healthier. Happy people live longer. Happy people are more likely to marry and tend to stay married longer. Happy people have more close friends and casual friends, and they earn more money. And there's even more good news for leaders—happy people win out in the workplace with better organizational citizenship, performance evaluations, and increased productivity.[14]

Happiness and life satisfaction are available to the young and the old, women and men, blacks and whites, the rich and the working-class.[15] This means you can have happiness and life satisfaction and all of the benefits that happy people experience. The happiness-success link exists not only because success makes people happy but also because positive affect engenders success. Although you might think you will be happy after you achieve success, happiness actually precedes success. *Positivity* opens the door to a whole new set of beneficial emotional resources, which in turn strengthens your energy to achieve goals.[16]

What amazing, wonderful news! Before you achieve your goals, meet the love of your life, or find the perfect ministry opportunity, a positive

THE POWER OF YOUR POSITIVE PERSPECTIVE

mind-set can create happiness in your life. The apostle Paul wrote, *"Rejoice in the Lord always. I will say it again: Rejoice!"* (Phil. 4:4). He knew that if you elevate your focus toward God's unlimited abundance you'll reinforce your happiness mind-set. Paul encouraged his readers to rejoice in the Lord always, meaning in every circumstance, to create a positive reality. When I talk about a positive reality, I'm not talking about one in which good things happen magically with the sheer power of positive thinking. Your positive reality is one in which you can summon your cognitive, intellectual, and emotional resources to create positive change because you *believe* change is possible.

> You can choose to think thoughts that are emotionally destructive and energy depleting, or you can elevate your life by choosing healing positive thoughts.

Philippians 4:8–9 gives us the key to happiness. We are to focus our attention on any shred of positivity. True leaders have an uncanny way to engage people in their mission or vision through contagious optimism—sometimes even unwarranted optimism. For these leaders, the glass is not half-full, it's running over with abundance and opportunity. The leaders I've studied and coached believe they can change the world, or at least they believe they're making a dent in the universe![17]

MANAGE YOUR TALKING

Here is what works for me: I revolutionize my attitude by consciously managing my talking. I only choose to use words that reflect God's purposes in my life. My words direct my thoughts. My thoughts produce my emotions. My emotions produce my decisions. My decisions produce my actions. My actions produce my habits. My habits produce my character. My character produces my destiny.[18]

words
↓
thoughts
↓
emotions
↓
decisions
↓
actions
↓
habits
↓
character
↓
destiny

True leaders have an uncanny way to engage people in their mission or vision through contagious optimism—sometimes even unwarranted optimism.

I can't keep moving forward without passion. My passion is only sustainable in my willingness to simply quit asking why and instead stand in faith on God's promise that I'm His daughter, walking a path He planned, "[living the good life which He prearranged and made ready for] [Robyn]" (Eph. 2:10, AMP).

Sometimes, we run into a situation or relationship issue where we have trouble seeing the positive. When that happens, we have to reframe the situation. This means looking at it from a different perspective. Eleanor Longden did just that when faced with an impossible situation in her life.

WHY I THANK THE VOICES IN MY HEAD

A beautiful, healthy young woman full of potential and headed to college, Eleanor Longden[19] started hearing voices in her head. Initially innocuous, these internal voices took on personalities, and became increasingly antagonistic and dictatorial, turning her life into a living nightmare. Every day, an abusive, authoritative, middle-aged male voice would spew messages into her mind: you aren't good enough; why bother to try, you're already a failure. Except Eleanor wouldn't listen.

Written off as a hopeless case, her devastated family found a psychiatrist who diagnosed her with schizophrenia. She was hospitalized and forced to take high doses of powerful hypnotic medication. For more than ten years she battled the voices in her head. However, Eleanor refused to allow herself to be defined by what was seen as an irreversible psychological limitation.

Today she declares herself recovered and is thankful for the voices in her head. Instead of being drugged and institutionalized, Eleanor is a speaker and researcher in the field of mental illness. How did she do it? By *reframing her illness*. She turned her situation around and looked at it from the opposite perspective. Instead of doing what patients normally do, Eleanor chose to try to understand what the voices could mean to her.

Her physician talked about recovery and encouraged her to try to listen to the voices rather than attempt to drown them out with drugs. They worked to reduce the medication, allowing Eleanor to think more clearly. Over time, she began to connect previous traumatic experiences with the messages the voices were speaking.

Eleanor also discovered the voices were worse when she was overtired and stressed. With her physician, she demonstrated that hearing voices in her head was not proof of schizophrenia but "a creative and genius survival strategy."[20] Eleanor tells the moving story of her decade-long journey back to mental health and makes the case that it was through learning to listen to her voices that she was able to survive.

Despite what traditional physicians may still think today, Eleanor Longden isn't crazy—and neither are many other patients who are hearing voices inside their heads. Eleanor spent many years in the psychiatric system before earning bachelor of science and master of science degrees in psychology, which are the highest classifications ever granted by the University of Leeds, England. Today she is studying for her PhD, and lectures and writes about recovery-oriented approaches to psychosis, dissociation, and complex trauma.[21]

By turning the problem around and seeing it from the opposite perspective, Eleanor found a way to actually harness the energy of her internal voices and make them work *for* her. She reframed how she viewed her illness. No one had ever talked to Eleanor about getting well. No one had ever dared to speak about recovery from schizophrenia, but today Eleanor is thankful for those crazy voices, and generations of people to come will forever be grateful as her breakthroughs continue to bring healing to psychiatric patients.

The ability to reframe virtually any issue into a positive attribute establishes an atmosphere of acceptance and cooperation rather than one of expert and subject. Genuinely accepting that every person's ideas, attitudes, and behaviors are positive and useful opens one's own perceptions to the potential rather than the limitations of any situation.

People who are more realistic (less optimistic) are accurate in their assessments of objective reality, but are less happy and don't live as long as people who choose to be optimistic.[22] Often a person who is a great optimistic reframer is discredited as being a "Pollyanna" and criticized for being naïve. In actuality, it would appear the Pollyanna optimism and naïve perceptions are actually more life-sustaining than those of the realist.

Reframing is vital for strong leadership. More than a technique to resolve a difficulty, reframing is an operating system for leaders. Once it becomes a habit, you'll see the whole world and everyone in it in terms of "what is right" rather than "what is wrong." If a leader wants to be successful at learning to reframe difficult situations, she must develop flexibility to make room for change.

FLEXIBILITY

Without change, growth is impossible. Leaders have more trouble than anybody else when it comes to receiving feedback. People tend to withhold important information from senior leaders, especially when it is unpleasant. Sometimes leaders don't encourage feedback, not because they're egotistic but because they genuinely believe they can't change.

Change means movement. Movement means friction. Change is letting go of things that are familiar and comfortable, even though they may not be good for us. Some people view change as a threat, not as a challenge or an opportunity. Some view change as exciting and invigorating. Most people don't initiate change, especially when things are going smoothly. It takes wisdom to know when to make changes. We need anchors that provide stability when change occurs.

Breaking the routine means being strong enough to be flexible. What happened to your spontaneity? At what moment did you lose the choice to do something new? Be intentional in your willingness to accept change by deliberately taking these steps:

- Think about the change
- Intend to do something about it
- Take action

Being willing to do things unlike your "normal" self is a way to treat yourself to a surprise. Escape the treadmill of predictability in every part of your life. You might:

- Wear bright clothes.
- Drive home a different route.
- Listen to different music—change the station on your radio.
- Walk outside for lunch and feed the birds.
- Call an old friend and say something affirming about an old experience together.

Before you move into the coaching in the next chapter, take a few moments to control your thoughts. Sit quietly, take a few deep breaths, and make sure you're in a positive frame of mind. Let's move forward! What can you do right now to be spontaneous and positive for your future?

THINGS TO CONSIDER:

1. Look at the three action steps from God at the beginning of this chapter. Explain how you can apply those steps to your life right now.

    - keep in my mind daily the end goal of eternity, not allowing myself to get caught up in worldly success.

    - Don't look at myself how the world views me but how God views me.

2. What steps can you take today to create your positive reality by using your cognitive, intellectual, and emotional resources?

    - Don't dwell on hard things

    - Use self-control w/ emotions

    - Practice possitivity.

3. If you were to start consciously managing your talking today, what changes do you think would happen in your life?

    - I already have and my resentment / bitterness has changed a lot. Now I need self-confidence

4. What changes can you make in your life to "escape the treadmill of predictability"?

    - Change up my free time

    - Enjoy little things / pay attention

    - Slow down, be still more.

5. Sit quietly, take a few deep breaths, and make sure you're in a positive frame of mind. Focus on what you can do right now to be spontaneous and positive for your future

CHAPTER NINE

COACHING: CHANGE IS POSSIBLE

Never lose an opportunity of urging a practical beginning, however small, for it is wonderful how often in such matters the mustard-seed germinates and roots itself.

—FLORENCE NIGHTINGALE

Our goal in this coaching section is not to fix what is broken but to uncover new talents and new ways to use old talents that will lead to greater leadership effectiveness.

COACHING EXERCISE: MY SOUNDING BOARD

Say this out loud: "As I turn my thinking around, I break free in a new direction toward my solution." Now create your own personal board of directors. How do you create one? You've already written a mission statement that reflects the goals you want to achieve over the next two to five years. Now identify five to seven people you would like to sit on your advisory board.

This must be a group of people you trust to give honest feedback on everything that matters to you. If part of your personal mission is to develop a new skill in the next two years, you want to make sure your board includes both personal and ministry friends. Remember, professional athletes surround themselves with the best players they can find. Pick people who are smarter than you and whose experience and knowledge are complementary to you and your goal. Now, write down the names of your new board and call them immediately to invite their support.

Convene your board once a year. Set aside a day to go over your personal goals and make time to discuss your goals with the individuals you have put on your board. The purpose is to organize people in your life you can rely on for honest, unflinching advice who will hold you accountable for your goals, and who are committed to helping you be the best you can be. Ask them how they see you. Are you perceived as generally positive or negative? Ask them to give you examples.

COACHING EXERCISE: THINK OUTSIDE OF THE BOX

To raise your awareness that you are able to choose to think differently: Connect the nine dots using four straight lines without lifting your pencil from the paper:

How did you do? Did it feel impossible? Nope. You can find the solution on page 123.

COACHING EXERCISE: WHAT AM I TOLERATING?

Women certainly have learned to tolerate a lot! We put up with, take on, and are dragged down by other people's behavior, situations, unmet needs, crossed boundaries, incompletions, frustrations, problems, and even our behavior. You are tolerating more than you might be aware.

Stop now and begin to think: *What am I tolerating?* As you become aware of things, write them down. Just raising your awareness by articulating each will bring them to the forefront of your mind. You will naturally start handling, eliminating, fixing, growing through, and resolving these tolerations. Enjoy this exercise!

1. The high expectations of others
2. High expectations for myself
3. Judgementalism / burdens of what the world says about women
4. Taking on more than I should
5. Giving up my dreams for others
6. _____
7. _____
8. _____
9. _____
10. _____

COACHING QUESTIONS: REFRAME

Reframing is the ability to create a reality in which all things are possible! A "transformissional" woman leader can change her perspective on how she is experiencing events, ideas, concepts, or emotions to find a more positive alternative that will help her move ahead, adapt, and implement solutions for achieving goals. Choosing a different perspective is essential to problem-solving, decision-making, and learning.

By reframing, you can summon all your cognitive, intellectual, and emotional resources to create positive change because you *believe* that positive change is possible. To move forward, you can increase your power to *reframe* every part of your life on the positive pathway toward your solution.

These coaching questions require honest answers. No one can know the story inside your thoughts, but even if your thoughts are negative today, you can switch your toxic thinking to positive power thoughts. Start by reading, thinking, meditating, praying, then writing out your answers. Apply the questions to your present life. Don't rehash yesterday—ask these questions with future solutions in mind.

1. When you are confronted with challenges, how do you focus on a solution?
2. Is that a story or the truth?
3. Are you acting on faith or fear?
4. What are you pretending not to know?
5. What are the three biggest changes you want to make in your life over the next five years?
6. What have been your three greatest workplace successes to date?
7. What obstacles do you see in your way?
8. What are your key stressors? On a scale of 1–10, how stressed are you right now?
9. What else could you do to support your ministry goals?
10. What else could you do to support your personal goals?
11. How do you respond when you're up against a wall?
12. What steps could you take immediately that would make the greatest difference in your current situation?
13. What are you most afraid of?
14. What coaching would you give yourself?
15. What is your current attitude?
16. In what way(s) are you sabotaging yourself and your goals?
17. What is holding you back from moving forward?
18. Whom do you have *to become* to achieve what you want to achieve?
19. What has to be modified in you?
20. What changes need to take place in your thinking?
21. What new knowledge do you need to gain?
22. How can you raise your level of new skills? What do you need to learn?

23. Is your self-talk positive or negative?
24. How do you choose to be with servant leaders, positive or negative?
25. How do you feel around negative people?
26. How do you feel around positive people?
27. Do you sense any physical changes around negative people? What are they?
28. Do you sense any physical changes around positive people? What are they?
29. What is an example of your negative talk?
30. How can you replace this with positive thoughts?
31. Everyone has energy highs and lows. When is the best time of day to reflect on your self-talk?
32. Is the cup half-full or half-empty?
33. Do you see a cloudy day with some sun or a sunny day with some clouds?
34. What changes do you need to make in how you see ministry?
35. What do you choose to be today, positive or negative?
36. Are you open to change?
37. How do you generally tend to focus—positive or negative? Why?
38. When and what do you waste the most time on?
39. What do you waste the most energy on?
40. What gives you energy?
41. If you could change one thing for people everywhere living today, what would it be?
42. What has your intuition been saying to you?
43. What have you been resisting?
44. What belief about yourself would be hardest for you to let go of?
45. What "shoulds" are you ready to drop?
46. What drains you?
47. What are you tolerating in your workplace, your home, your body, your relationships?
48. Energy is vital. When and how do you lose emotional energy?
49. To make emotional energy your top priority, what do you have to change?

50. Your focused attention is your mind-set. How can you make your mind-set a positive, creative force?
51. What takes up your thinking time?
52. How do your thoughts make your life more stressful, or less stressful?
53. What do you participate in that is toxic to your mind-set?
54. What is the first change you would like to make to be fully satisfied with your life?
55. Where in your life do you know you need to make improvements?
56. What changes would make the biggest difference to your life?
57. To have less stress in your life, what needs to go?
58. To have more joy in your life, what needs to change?
59. Who can help you achieve your leadership goals?
60. What things are you regularly doing that don't support your goals?
61. For you to be truly happy, what would you have to change?

POSITIVE POWER PRAYER: COACHING FROM THE INSIDE OUT

Reframing begins with your belief in God's desire to bless you. Paul wrote, "And God will generously provide all you need. Then you will always have everything you need and plenty left over to share with others" (2 Cor. 9:8, NLT). You have the *choice* to reframe your thoughts to seek out God's goodness in every situation—no matter what. By habitually bringing your thoughts into captivity and focusing on God's Word you will increase your awareness of the Holy Spirit at work in your life.

Focused attention is like a muscle that you can strengthen through exercise. Begin with a prayer of thanksgiving. *Be grateful* for where you are in life today. Read one Scripture out loud and insert your first name into the sentence. As you speak the Scripture, declare the promise and reframe your circumstances into a positive outcome with a hopeful future. Stop. Now, do it again. Your faith is created as you envision yourself living in your amazing future. By reframing your perspective on all circumstances

COACHING: CHANGE IS POSSIBLE

you are breaking free to move your mind in a positive direction. As you think through your reframing process, focus on these Scriptures and speak to your future:

- "For I know the plans I have for you [_____]," declares the Lord, "plans to prosper you and not to harm you, plans to give you hope and a future." (Jer. 29:11)
- A happy heart [_____] is good medicine and a joyful mind causes healing, but a broken spirit dries up the bones. (Prov. 17:22, AMP)
- We know that all things work together for the good of those who love God—those whom he has called according to his plan. This is true because he already knew his people and had already appointed them [_____] to have the same form as the image of his Son. Therefore, his Son is the firstborn among many children. (Rom. 8:28–29, GW)
- Be careful how you think [_____]; your life is shaped by your thoughts. (Prov. 4:23, GNT)
- [_____] Do all things without grumbling or disputing. (Phil. 2:14, ESV)
- When someone does something bad to you, do not do the same thing to him. When someone talks about you, do not talk about him. Instead, [_____] pray that good will come to him. You were called to do this so you [_____] might receive good things from God. (1 Peter 3:9, NLV)
- Thoughtless words [_____] can wound as deeply as any sword, but wisely spoken words can heal. (Prov. 12:18, GNT)
- Worry can rob you [_____] of happiness, but kind words will cheer you up. (Prov. 12:25, GNT)
- [_____] Church helpers must also have a good character and be sincere. (1 Tim. 3:8, GNT)
- My thoughts will be clear; I [_____] will speak words of wisdom. (Ps. 49:3, GNT)
- A soft and gentle and thoughtful answer [_____] turns away

wrath, but harsh and painful and careless words stir up anger. (Prov. 15:1, AMP)

- Jesus said to them, "Have faith in God. I tell you the truth, if someone says to this mountain, 'Be lifted up and thrown into the sea,' and does not doubt in his heart but believes that what he says will happen, it will be done for him. For this reason I tell you [_____], whatever you pray and ask for, believe that you have received it, and it will be yours. Whenever you stand praying, if you [_____] have anything against anyone, forgive him, so that your Father in heaven will also forgive you your sins." (Mark 11:22–25, NET)

- We [_____] break down every thought and proud thing that puts itself up against the wisdom of God. We take hold of every thought and make it obey Christ. (2 Cor. 10:5, NLV)

- [_____] Stop being mean, bad-tempered, and angry. Quarreling, harsh words, and dislike of others should have no place in your lives. Instead, be kind to each other, tenderhearted, forgiving one another, just as God has forgiven you because you belong to Christ. (Eph. 4:31–32, TLB)

- What you say [_____] can preserve life or destroy it; so you must accept the consequences of your words. (Prov. 18:21, GNT)

- "And whatever you [_____] ask in prayer, you will receive, if you have faith." (Matt. 21:22, ESV)

- I [_____] can do all things through him who strengthens me. (Phil. 4:13, ESV)

- [_____] Don't worry about anything, but pray about everything. With thankful hearts offer up your prayers and requests to God. Then, because you [_____] belong to Christ Jesus, God will bless you with peace that no one can completely understand. And this peace will control the way you think and feel. (Phil. 4:6–7, CEV)

- [_____] The wise speak, presenting knowledge appropriately, but fools spout foolishness. (Prov. 15:2, ISV)

- If you [_____] do nothing in a difficult time, your strength is limited. (Prov. 24:10, HCSB)

- So [_____] if you're serious about living this new resurrection life with Christ, act like it. Pursue the things over which Christ presides. Don't shuffle along, eyes to the ground, absorbed with the things right in front of you. Look up, [_____] and be alert to what is going on around Christ—that's where the action is. See things from his perspective. (Col. 3:1–2, MSG)

- May my [_____'s] words and my thoughts be acceptable to you, O LORD, my refuge and my redeemer! (Ps. 19:14, GNT)

- And we know that God causes everything to work together for the good of those [_____] who love God and are called according to his purpose for them. (Rom 8:28, NLT)

- [_____] A person's words can be a source of wisdom, deep as the ocean, fresh as a flowing stream. (Prov. 18:4, GNT)

- Finally, believers, [_____] whatever is true, whatever is honorable and worthy of respect, whatever is right and confirmed by God's Word, whatever is pure and wholesome, whatever is lovely and brings peace, whatever is admirable and of good repute; [_____] if there is any excellence, if there is anything worthy of praise, think continually on these things [center your mind on them, and implant them in your heart]. (Phil. 4:8, AMP)

THINK OUTSIDE THE BOX SOLUTION

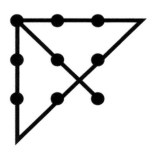

PART 3

LEADERSHIP ATTRIBUTE: CONNECTING

Love is a fruit in season at all times, and within reach of every hand.

—MOTHER TERESA

ATTRIBUTE AFFIRMATION:
WHAT I MAKE HAPPEN FOR OTHERS,
GOD WILL MAKE HAPPEN FOR ME.

CHAPTER TEN

COLLABORATION FROM THE INSIDE OUT

Often, even the thought of risking, trusting, trying, engaging again
in any organized context feels too overwhelming. But part of moving
forward as we rebuild our faith is exploring possibilities for community and
connection.

—KATHY ESCOBAR

Leadership gives a church or an organization a vision and the ability to
create a reality around a shared mission. However, the problem with many
organizations is that they are overmanaged and under-led. There is the
difference between management and leadership. To "manage" means to bring
about or succeed in accomplishing something. However, "to lead" is defined
as "the initiative in an action; an example for others to follow."

The difference is vital to understanding what is required for you to be
the leader you want to be. Managers are women who do things right, but
leaders are women who do the right thing. The difference between the
two can be summarized as a manager mastering actions of routine, while
the leader is conquering activities of vision and judgment so she can be
effective. Leadership requires certain traits, some of which you are born
with and some you develop. The ability to connect with those around you
is one of those traits.

THE TRAITS OF A LEADER

"You are *not* going to take Vanessa and Zachary to Miami! You are not about to leave Naperville for some foolish idea to pastor in Miami in 'the hood'! You're a highly educated, Ivy League graduate, environmental engineer, and you're going to drop your life career for that little church? I'm totally opposed to the idea! I don't agree! It's crazy!"

As an African American woman leader who was trained as a nurse, a teacher, and a graduate of Columbia University, Linda's mother was firmly confident that Linda and her husband, David, were making a huge mistake. She had worked very hard to put herself through college when most women in the United States weren't even thinking of higher education. She had achieved what many thought was impossible. So now, after all her sacrifice, why would her attractive, brilliant, eldest daughter choose to drag her two children and husband down to Miami to work in some tiny, inner-city church? It made absolutely no sense to her.

An engineer, Linda Freeman was working her way up through the ranks of federal employment as an environmental project manager. Her computer-engineer husband, David, also enjoyed success in his field of custom code development. Her mom was right. Everything was perfect for them in Naperville. The kids were thriving in Calvary Church Christian School, their jobs were lucrative, and as a family everything was going great.

But Linda had felt the call of God in her heart. Through servant leadership, she had activated the adventure of ministry by enlisting in her church's missions construction teams. Linda traveled overseas many times with team members, bringing medical, construction, and educational services to people in need. In January of 1999, Linda signed up to work in Miami at Trinity Church. Upon arriving, she and her team were stunned to find themselves sleeping on raw concrete floors inside the church and waking to cockroaches scurrying over their sleeping bags. The place was a mess. Back-breaking work seemed endless and impossible. Linda was shocked to realize that all this work was needed in a United States church in an American city. This was not unlike what she had witnessed overseas.

Over several years of preaching regularly at Calvary Church in Naperville, my husband had met Linda and Dave. Whenever he would see them, he would jokingly admonish the couple that someday they would work with him. Now Linda found herself in Miami, on her missions team, working with Pastor Rich and attempting to launch a new work in the inner city. It was Super Bowl weekend, and NFL football star Reggie White was the guest in the big tent erected on the church parking lot. Thousands came and hundreds answered the altar calls. Linda was compelled.

With resolve in her heart to obey God's call on her life, Linda flew home, talked to her husband and one of her pastors, and together she and David made the decision to move to Miami. With no salary, no place to live, no moving vans, and no certainty of what the future held, Linda and Dave set out for Miami. For the first full year they slept on the floor in an apartment, working and believing for provision. By rolling up her sleeves, Linda started the Peacemakers Family Center, serving the underserved neighborhoods surrounding the church campus. She worked to organize services and create a safe place for people in need.

With Linda's strong background in project management and a vision for missions, she began to develop much-needed programs and services for our church community. As the executive director, she has won more than forty million dollars in contracts and grants for Peacemakers Family Service Center, and she continues to lead overseas missions trips with new creative strategies for sustainable community development.

Although Pastor Linda can report amazing professional victories, what does she quickly describe as her greatest achievement so far? "The best gift God ever gave me is my family!" as she refers to her children and family. Both of her kids are Christians, college graduates, and both are following in their parents' footsteps through servant leadership. Linda's son, Zachary Freeman, is a worship pastor. Her daughter, Vanessa, is preparing to begin her residency as a physician serving in the United States Army, with a specialty in psychiatry.

Women in leadership serve in ministry with kids and families watching. Those little hearts grow up witnessing the thrill of evangelism and the transformational power of discipleship up close and personal. Pastor

Linda leads today with missional energy, reframing her obstacles for her most valuable reality, connecting with hundreds of other community initiatives, but all the while being renewed in the power of the Holy Spirit. Linda's mom now lives with David and Linda in Miami, enjoying the Florida sunshine. When asked what she thinks about Trinity Church now, she answers quickly, "Oh, I always knew Linda was destined to be a great pastor!"

Linda exemplifies the characteristics of a strong female leader, but her ability to connect with others is what makes her so inspirational to those around her. She excels at building and creating relationships and finds great satisfaction from those relationships. Relationships are the single most important influence on happiness. In fact, friendships are more than a chance to hang out, and romantic relationships are more than just sexual attraction. Social relationships can be understood as social capital that improves performance at work and creates a foundation for a solid home life. In every part of life, good relationships are important because they lead to effective work and living.

Relationships also mean helping others maximize their God-given potential. Potential is God's gift to you. What you do with it is your gift back to God. After coaching someone to unveil their God-given gifts and calling, my greatest satisfaction as a parent, pastor, or friend is watching them operate in their strengths. Before I can start that coaching process, however, I have to connect with them. As a leader, you must be able to connect with those around you, deal successfully with conflict, and build trust.

CONNECTIVITY

Connectivity is a range of activities that focus on creating and sustaining connections with others. Historically, leadership has been viewed as a singular pursuit; a process undertaken by the individual.[2] A more modern perspective of leadership is one in which leadership "is something that is occurring between people, groups, and systems."[3] Sound familiar? No leader operates alone, especially women leaders. You need that connection with others if you want to lead effectively.

Connected leadership will link you to your followers. As a positive side effect, connectivity will help build your organization or church from the inside out! What you need are specific actions you can take to ensure connectivity happens. An attitude of servant leadership is the first thing you need to enhance and improve your ability to connect with others in a constructive, purposeful, and meaningful way.

Servant leadership focuses on the development of altruism, emotional

> No leader operates alone, especially women leaders. You need that connection with others if you want to lead effectively.

healing, wisdom, support, and stewardship.[4] This foundation facilitates empowerment and capability development, leading to a sense of community and an alignment of goals.[5]

You must change the way you view leadership, recognizing that it isn't an individualistic pursuit. As a leader, you are participating in an interactive process involving hands-on action, and you must make an effort to include all stakeholders in the process.[6] Communicating, listening, integrating viewpoints, taking action, and building trust are all critical to your success.[7]

If you don't already possess it, or even if you think you do, work on your ability to be a good listener. Be sensitive toward others, and give and take criticism graciously. Solid people skills will take you farther toward professional success than any other leadership trait! Or as President Theodore Roosevelt put it, "The most important single ingredient in the formula of success is knowing how to get along with people."

Jesus recognized the need to view leadership in a different light when He chose the role of a servant. He also demonstrated a foundation for equality in His actions, choosing to wash the feet of His followers. He demonstrated the importance of serving others and the equality in the roles they shared (John 13:12–15).

When you lead as Jesus did, you can't expect that you'll receive reward or recognition.[8] If you want to influence the behavior of others, and create a network of positive connectivity, you have to abandon that mind-set.[9] This is the lesson Jesus taught through His actions.[10] "Leaders who change the world decide, up front, to put more into life than they ever hope to take out of it."[11] You are a leader who can change the world! So are you capable of accepting your role as a servant to meet the needs of others?

DEALING WITH CONFLICT

Admittedly, servanthood, a "servolution," requires innovation.

> This means thinking about who is not being targeted and who is falling through the cracks, then getting creative about meeting those needs. It's giving and serving with no strings attached. And yes, it means serving them even if they will never set foot inside your church. If we focus our energies on simply meeting the needs of God's people, we believe we will never need to worry about the growth of our church.[12]

Part of connecting with and serving others is dealing with conflict. Your effectiveness often depends on teamwork, a sense of unity, purpose, direction, and vision that propels you forward and enables you to work in harmony with others toward a common goal. When conflicts come up and aren't resolved, both you and your organization or church can suffer. Your followers can lose trust in your abilities if your goals and vision don't align. This division can separate you from other leaders, disrupting effectiveness when you can no longer act with confidence that your followers will work with you in harmony.

Have you ever been in a situation where you were reluctant to work with certain followers, favoring closeness with known allies over others? This further contributes to the division. When that happens, your followers become discouraged or even derisive. This starts a cycle of bad decisions, less positive action, and more division. Conflict in your team can significantly undermine the church or organization as a whole. It's

COLLABORATION FROM THE INSIDE OUT

vital that you learn to deal with conflict!

We've all been there. A member of your team starts making a bid for power, protecting the duties they "own," and trying to control every situation to their benefit. This is antagonism at its finest, and it's devastating to your leadership because of the importance of Christian love as the foundation for everything you do. When antagonists stir conflict, they gather allies who agree with their position.[13] Their actions are a poison like gangrene, and the poison eventually spreads throughout the body. Negative conflict occurs because of negative emotions, incompatibilities between people, competitiveness, and defensive behaviors.[14]

> When conflicts come up and aren't resolved, both you and your organization or church can suffer.

If you don't deal with conflict, it will affect the heart, personal relationships, and the soul. The heart can become bitter and resentful as unforgiveness takes root. Unforgiveness arises when you harbor ill will toward another person, and it quickly leads to a negative attitude.[15] You'll eventually express the bitterness in your heart in some way that hurts others. Hebrews 12:15 tells us to, "See to it that . . . no bitter root grows up to cause trouble and defile many."[16] Even good desires, when they become demands, lead to bitterness and conflict. These desires can become idols that replace the love of God and others as what is most important.

Anyone who is willing to put an idea, a desire, or a concern above the love they feel for their fellow Christians can't express the love Jesus taught and embraced as the foundation of Christian life and practice. As a leader, you need to create a loving, supportive, trusting environment (1 Cor. 13:13). When there are conflicts with others, true freedom ceases to exist. The soul itself is injured.

Life is comprised of six components: thought, feeling, body, social relationships, spirit/will, and soul.[17] These frame the human identity, not only in terms of the self but in terms of relationships with God and others. Loving God and others is critical to human life. Without harmony in your relationships with other people, an important aspect of the self is unfulfilled and hurting. Without harmony in your relationship with God, you can never feel fulfilled and whole. Your leadership will suffer, your followers will suffer, and you will suffer.

POWER OF PARTNERSHIP

"I'm out of here! There's no way I'm going back into that office. That woman is crazy, and I'm not going to take it anymore. I called my husband and he says he'll help me pay the rent until I can find another job. I won't be spoken to like that ever again. I'm sick of it!"

Susie had stormed into my office in the middle of the day, and she was sobbing and screaming at me at the same time. "I can't get along with her. She tells me to do one thing, and then she changes her mind. I don't know how to please her. Why can't she just change?" I exhaled as I knew that this mother of three was now on her last nerve with her coworker. Finding a way to smooth over personality conflict is an important part of your leadership at home and at work. Giving encouragement while working out new ways to build teamwork is critical to accomplishing your goals.

I spoke calmly and slowly in a low voice, "Sit down. Exhale. You need your job and we need you. Let's not overreact to a situation we can resolve if we just look at things from a new perspective. How can we turn this argument around to be a bridge to solving the tension in your department?" Susie wouldn't hear it. She was done. Done! "I'm quitting right now. Consider this my resignation."

I wouldn't budge. "No way. You've overcome tremendous obstacles to be where you are in your career. You created the entire process for managing our paperwork; we need your expertise. What if you took the rest of today off, and tomorrow? Come back on Monday and let's start again. In the mean time, I'll meet with your coworker and together we'll find a resolution." She finally shrugged an affirmative reply and crept out of my office.

Immediately, I reached for the phone and contacted a professional organizational coach and described the situation to him. There was so much at stake. How could I lead this conflict into a new place where everyone on the team would win? He offered to help with interventions with everyone in the department over the telephone. Together we read a few books, took several personality assessments, and knocked out new procedures and job descriptions for everyone. The result? Three women in the department resigned and moved on, but the key players figured it out. Today, they lead our biggest and most efficient department as partners. There are miracles in the atmosphere of agreement. Abundance doesn't flourish in chaos, but when calm positive leadership gets traction everyone is a winner.

TRUST

Conflict becomes much easier to deal with when trust exists. The capacity to generate and maintain trust is the central ingredient to leadership.[18] Trust is the glue that holds your team together and knits you to your common success!

So how do we build trust, not only among our followers but also between ourselves and those we follow? By demonstrating competence, caring, and consistency.[19] Think about that. You are far more likely to trust in the abilities of someone who is good at what they do. The same goes for the people around you. If they see you are competent at what you do, they're more likely to trust you for your skills, knowledge, and abilities.[20]

As a Christian leader, caring should be central to everything you do. When you honestly care for those around you, they understand that they matter to you. This fosters a sense of camaraderie and builds trust much better than some of the "trust exercises" common in the corporate world!

You know that old adage, "Walk the walk, don't just talk the talk"? Well, it's wrong. You need to do both! Consistency means doing what you say you are going to do. When you are reliable, people know they can trust you. Trust is central to connecting with the people around you. It's necessary for successful relationships, makes you a stronger leader, and allows others to buy into your vision.

CARING

Often we can't remember what a person said, but we always remember how that person made us feel. This quiz has been all around the world on the web illustrating what truly makes a difference in life. Take the next few moments to see how you do:

1. Name the five wealthiest people in the world.
2. Name the last five Heisman Trophy winners.
3. Name the last five winners of the Miss America contest.
4. Name five people who have won the Nobel or Pulitzer Prize.
5. Name the five "Most Valuable Players" of the World Series.

Here's the point: Even though the individuals mentioned above are world class in their professions, we don't remember the headliners of yesterday. Applause dies, awards tarnish, and achievements are quickly forgotten.

Now try this quiz:

1. List five teachers who aided your journey through school.
2. Name five friends or family members who have helped you through a difficult time.
3. List five people who have taught you something important.
4. Name five people who have made you feel appreciated, or valued.
5. List five heroes whose stories have inspired you.

Was that second quiz much easier? The lesson is simple: The people who make a difference in the lives of those around them are the ones who are the *true* leaders. They are the ones who care.

COLLABORATION FROM THE INSIDE OUT

THINGS TO CONSIDER:

1. Think of a part of your life where you manage instead of lead. What can you do to shift into leadership?

    — Core help? I don't know how to change that though

    — Marriage, at times

2. How can servant leadership help you form stronger connections in your life?

    —Willingness to sacrifice speaks volumes

3. List three actions you can take to become a better listener.

    • Keep eyes focused on person

    • Try to retain all information

    • Don't let my mind wander

4. Have you ever been in a situation where you were reluctant to work with certain followers, favoring closeness with known allies over others? How can you deal with situations like this as a leader?

    — Purposefully list the good qualities of each person & write down the potential I see in them.

5. How can you build trust in your life?

    — Become more consistent

    — Notice what others do for me.

CHAPTER ELEVEN

SERVANT LEADERSHIP

At the end of these days I bend next to the bed and I ask only that I could bend more, bend lower. Because I serve a Savior who came to be a servant, . . . the more I bend the harder and better and fuller this life gets. And sure, we are tired, but oh we are happy. Because bent down low is where we find fullness of Joy.

—KATIE J. DAVIS

We believe that our mission to Miami is Christ's mission to humankind: to reach outside our church building walls to everyone in need (outreach); to practice generosity and invest resources into the social needs of our community (compassion); and to practice faith by living fearlessly (abundance). "He who is greatest among you shall be your servant. And whoever exalts himself will be humbled, and he who humbles himself will be exalted" (Matt. 23:11–12, NKJV). Another version says, "The person who is greatest among you will be your servant. Whoever honors himself will be humbled, and whoever humbles himself will be honored" (GW). These words of Jesus describe leadership from God's point of view.

During Jesus' lifetime in first-century Palestine, authority and power were the means to maintain civil order. The Romans ruled with ruthless pomp and authority across the ancient world. It must have been an awesome sight to see the Roman centurions and their soldiers marching through the streets of Jerusalem or Capernaum, ready to enforce their will. It filled the people with fear. With authority came influence, prestige, and position. By way of contrast, servants and slaves were on the opposite end of the social order. They existed for the benefit of others, with no rights or protection from abuse. They lived at the bottom of the social hierarchy. From the normal human point of view, who wouldn't rather be a ruler than a servant?

Jesus spoke many times of a different kind of leadership, usually ending with a summary, "Anyone who wants to be first must be the very last, and the servant of all" (Mark 9:35). "But I am among you as one who serves" (Luke 22:27). "Whoever wants to become great among you must be your servant, and whoever wants to be first must be your slave—just as the Son of Man did not come to be served, but to serve, and to give his life as a ransom for many" (Matt. 20:26–28). "The greatest among you will be your servant" (Matthew 23:11).

STARTING OVER

"What do you mean when you say my moving truck burned to the ground? How could such a thing happen? You're saying that everything in that truck is gone? Everything?" Pastor Kathie heard herself yelling into the phone.

"Yes ma'am. The driver reported to us that his truck caught flames and he had to pull over to the side of the road. By the time he could get help to extinguish the fire the entire truck was engulfed in flames. We're so sorry. We have one box of items retrieved from the fire for you."

Kathie couldn't believe her ears. The moving company representative was attempting to sound calm and convincing. Days earlier the truck transporting all her household goods—including furniture—from Sacramento to Miami had caught fire in the Nevada desert.

"Okay, well I guess I just have to exhale now and try to think. This means that all my dishes, my clothes, my kids' stuff, our furniture, linens, photos, books, family heirlooms and keepsakes from twenty years of marriage are all gone?"

"Yes, Kathie. Everything's gone."

So what happened next? Kathie and her husband, Greg, sat down together and rejoiced! Yes, they cried a little, too. But the overarching family version of this event is that the journey from Sacramento business life to Miami, inner-city missionary life softened the blow when the truck never arrived. Moving by faith from California to Miami was energizing for Kathie because of her calling to ministry. When asked how she felt about the loss of all her household belongings, Kathie answered, "Of course, I'm grieving many of the precious items on that truck. No, they weren't worth anything to others, but many were irreplaceable, priceless mementos for me. But here's the thing. We moved here to answer God's call.

"I've always been a servant leader working in our Sacramento church. But now that my three kids are grown, I'm ready for full-time work. I love children, and I love teaching. Here in Miami there's a serious high school dropout rate, especially here in our church neighborhood. Yes, I could retire and sit at the beach. I could go help my husband in his real estate development business, but the truth is I want my life to count for something *more*. I just want to matter!"

More than a decade later, Pastor Kathie Hardcastle leads Trinity Christian Academy at Trinity Church. Through her perseverance and determination, she has pioneered education ministries for thousands of children and their families in a high-risk urban community. Having earned her doctorate in education, Kathie has persevered with vision and purpose to see her mission accomplished in the lives of children. When you're on a mission to serve God and others, pain is processed through His calling on your life.

YOUR LEADERSHIP MODEL

Jesus is your model for leadership. He didn't measure greatness and power by the number of people who served a leader but by the willingness of the leader to serve those under him. "The greatest leaders are people who never set out to be leaders. True leaders don't elevate themselves."[1] At the beginning of His ministry, we see Jesus preparing to lead by acts of submission and testing of His character. In Matthew 3:13–17 and 4:1–11 we read two key interactions. "Then Jesus came from Galilee to the Jordan

Servant leaders never ask anyone to do something they aren't willing to do themselves.

to be baptized by John. But John tried to deter him, saying, 'I need to be baptized by you, and do you come to me?' Jesus replied, 'Let it be so now; it is proper for us to do this to fulfill all righteousness.' Then John consented." In His interaction with John, Jesus demonstrated two significant attributes of servant leadership: (1) He validated and affirmed John's ministry and (2) He submitted to the acts of surrender required of others. Servant leaders never ask anyone to do something they aren't willing to do themselves.

In reading Matthew 4:1–11, it's easy to concentrate on the physical hardships of Jesus' fast in the wilderness and miss the profound spiritual conditioning for servant leadership that took place. Jesus was tempted by three of the most universal and powerful leadership temptations: instant gratification, recognition, and the lust for power. However, He used the Word of God to confront and defeat the Devil. Spiritual preparation determines the quality of our service.

To more fully understand servant leadership, it might be easier to identify what it isn't as it pertains to your leadership, rather than what it is. It isn't a refuge for those without the willingness, ability, or courage to lead. I know you're willing and have courage because you're reading this, and you want to work on your ability. It isn't an excuse for failing to give direction and be accountable. As a leader, people will constantly call on you to give direction. You are accountable not only for your own actions, but for the actions of those you lead. Leadership isn't passive. You are called to be an *active* leader. It isn't simply doing what your followers want to do. You are a *leader*. That means you occasionally have to make decisions that aren't popular. It isn't necessarily keeping everyone happy. It isn't giving up your own personhood. In the story of the foot washing, Jesus knew "he had come from God and was returning to God" (John 13:3). He was deeply secure in His identity. Weakness didn't cause Him to be a servant; offering Himself to serve others came out of that strong self-image.[2] Being a servant doesn't mean you abdicate responsibility for leadership. Jesus also knew "that the Father had put all things under his power" (John 13:3). When you answered God's call to leadership, you accepted that leadership responsibility.

So what is servant leadership? Basically, it's being a servant and a leader at the same time. *Servant* defines the timeless, changeless style and attitude that must be present in your life. *Leadership* defines the responsibility. The journey of life is to move from a self-serving heart to a serving heart. You become a mature adult when you realize life is about what you give, rather than what you receive. Following Jesus as our model, we are all called to be servants. When you assume the responsibility of motivating people to bring about purposeful change, you must do so as a servant-leader. If you serve but don't lead, you may be a wonderful servant but you aren't a servant-leader. You are called to lead with diligence (Rom. 12:8). Jesus said, "The one who rules [should be] like the one who serves" (Luke 22:26). He didn't say the one who gives up ruling should be a servant, but the one who rules.[3]

GOD-GIVEN CALL

When God calls you to lead, you must lead. When He asks you to lead, you are responsible and accountable to lead, but it is a call that needs to be exercised in a *spirit* of serving. Leading is a way of serving. Leadership is not evil! Lack of leadership is chaos. The lack of leadership produces followers who are "harassed and helpless, like sheep without a shepherd" (Matt. 9:36). In God's kingdom, leaders serve us best by leading us and lead best by serving us.

Good leadership does at least two things: (1) It accomplishes worthwhile goals and (2) it develops and transforms those who are led. People are better people because they have served with you as their leader. They are more competent, confident, and equipped. Your leadership is necessary to transform vision into reality. "Servant leadership is not a different category of leadership but the style and attitude that pervades every method of Christian leadership."[4]

In God's kingdom, leaders serve us best by leading us and lead best by serving us.

At times, leaders can best serve their followers by leading autocratically (as when Jesus told His disciples what to take, do, and say on their first missionary venture in Matthew 10:5–16). Other times, the servant-leader leads democratically (as when Jesus asked the input of the disciples in the feeding of the five thousand in John 6:5). Other times, Jesus led best by allowing the disciples to figure things out on their own ("Go make disciples of all nations. . . ." Matt. 28:18–20). In each situation Jesus' method varied, but His style and attitude never changed.[5] Whatever He did, He did as a servant leader.

Your leadership also requires purpose and direction. Everything Jesus did, from His baptism to the cross, was laden with purpose. As a servant-leader, His vision was clear. As a servant-leader He said to His potential followers, "I know where I'm going. I want you to go with me, and I'll serve you by giving you what you need along the way." As a servant-leader He understood each disciple's giftedness, gave them work in line with their giftedness, held them accountable, and helped them with their weaknesses. He took time to explain, time and again, the goals of their mission.

To Jesus, servant leadership wasn't a program but a response. Yes, He washed the disciple's feet one time in response to a real need, but His primary duty was not foot washing. Jesus involved His disciples in the learning process. He helped them to be more effective and to become more efficient at what they did. The disciples who couldn't cast out demons in Matthew 17:14–20 were later quite successful at it (Acts 5:12–15). Jesus equipped His disciples to solve problems and make decisions in view of the stated mission. He was free to give the ministry away. The real test of His leadership was how well the disciples performed after His departure. It worked!

"Transformissional" leadership is servant leadership: "Do nothing out of selfish ambition or vain conceit. Rather, in humility value others above

yourselves, not looking to your own interests but each of you to the interests of others. In your relationships with one another, have the same mindset as Christ Jesus: Who, being in very nature God, . . . made himself nothing by taking the very nature of a servant, being made in human likeness" (Phil. 2:3–7). Regardless of the mode, the focus of servant leadership is on the growth, success, and welfare of the followers. This singular characteristic defines servant leadership. This is a focus you may find you need most when one of your team is in crisis.

FOLLOWING GOD'S CALL—NO MATTER WHAT

"He's leaving me for another woman! Here's my letter of resignation. I've tried to work from home but it's just not working. I quit." My assistant had just dropped a bombshell, and I was speechless. Now talking faster, she sat clinging to the other side of my desk and kept going. "I just think I've spent too much time here at the church. Being your assistant is overwhelming, and I can't go on." Silently, I kept looking at her. She continued, "Okay! So I can't lie to you . . . and I know you already know. You knew months ago, and I just didn't want to tell you. But yes! My husband has been having an affair for months. He met someone at his workplace . . . and he isn't going to give her up!"

I wouldn't accept my assistant's resignation, and together we prayed as we knew she was facing the trauma of divorce. Tears flowed as her heartbreak gushed out. Months earlier her husband had stated that the time she gave to her leadership at church made him unhappy. Shocked and humiliated by this, she had quit *everything*. She quit leading young couples in premarriage counseling and she quit working in the drama department to create incredible makeup for actors. She quit socializing with her many friends at church. That was months ago, and after all her efforts her husband was leaving her anyway.

They had met in grade school and had been friends most of their lives. As a teenager she was outgoing, popular at church, and adored by her Cuban parents and family. Having grown up in a loving Christian family,

Maria was secure and full of zest for life. Her Cuban boyfriend was shy but playful, tall, and handsome. They were in love. When they got married, Maria found her greatest calling to be a wife and mom. Their son was born and life was prosperous. However, Maria felt that she wanted to reach higher in her personal growth and development.

She knew she was called to leadership in ministry, and she found every area of church service exciting and energizing. Working as a servant-leader volunteer, and then later as the business administrator, Maria found her "passion for leadership zone" in ministry at the church. But something was lacking. When she looked in the mirror she knew she wasn't living her healthiest life. Having been overweight as a teenager, Maria made some drastic decisions to change her health. She lost more than one hundred pounds. At a petite five-foot-one, the brown-eyed, brunette found herself swimming in extra skin! Her physician recommended a "body lift" to surgically remove the excess skin from her tiny frame. Although it was a painful journey, Maria emerged from her cocoon a gorgeous butterfly. She just knew her young husband would love her new, healthy look. She felt better about herself than ever before, and she had done it mostly for him.

But it didn't work out that way. After all her efforts at being and doing her best for her husband, he was leaving her anyway. He wanted another woman. So what happened next? Did Maria fall apart and go on long weekend binges trying to find "love in all the wrong places" across the night life of South Beach? Did she quit serving God and stop ministering in the church she loved so much? Nope.

Instead, she sat down with herself and had a serious conversation with God. "Lord, I know You love my husband and I know You love me. Although he wants me not to get a divorce (while he lives this shocking lifestyle), I just can't stay in this marriage if he insists on having another woman. God, You know I love being married. You know I love being part of a family, but I also know You have planned for me to be blessed and to prosper. Staying in this adulterous marriage is going to kill me, so I must get a divorce. Today I'm going to stand on Your Word and believe for an amazing future for myself."

Do you know what Maria did next? Through tears falling across her notepad, she wrote out a *vision* for her future. Having moved out of her home and now sitting in her one-bedroom apartment, she started her paper with the heading, "My future, in Jesus' name, will be . . ." And then in faith she wrote out in detail her most outrageous requests. Maria wanted to be loved again by a faithful Christian husband, preferably Cuban. She wanted him to have a boat, and she wanted to live by the ocean. Next, she wanted to get married with a new wedding ring in the shape and design of the most recent fashion. With great description and detail she crafted a lengthy narrative of what she longed for. Next, she clutched the dream to her chest and prayed, "God, I know most people would think this is insane, but I'm crazy enough to trust Your great love for me. And just like I love my son, I'm Your daughter and I know You love me and want me to be happy. So I'm claiming this future in Jesus' name!"

Then she went shopping. As she walked through a department store, she noticed an off-white, raw silk dress hanging on a mannequin. She thought, *Wow, that dress would make a nice wedding dress for some happy bride!* Then all of a sudden it hit her! Hey! Why not me? That's my wedding dress! She found her size and rushed to the fitting room to try it on. To her amazement it fit like a glove. She felt beautiful—again. In that moment, looking in the mirror, she felt confident that God was answering her prayers, but she would have to take action to see them come into reality. She bought the dress and took it home to her tiny condo on the beach.

Although her husband had stayed in their house, their son would often come and spend nights with her. That evening, before sitting down for dinner, she showed Miguel her new dress. He quizzed her, "Wow, Mom, that's a beautiful dress. But, where are you going to wear it?" Her twenty-five-year-old son thought it seemed odd that his newly divorced mother would be going out somewhere fancy!

"Miguel, this is my wedding dress!" He laughed and shot a look at her like she might be going crazy and said, "What? No, really, what's it for?" She repeated herself and stated, "Miguel, I am taking action toward my goal. I'm going to place my dress at the entrance of my closet to remind me every day that God is going to answer my prayer. I'm standing in faith, knowing He will provide for even the deepest desires of my heart!

> You will uncover your destiny by walking joyfully and obediently in God's purpose for your life.

It's going to happen." Through many anxious, lonely nights of tears, Maria prayed herself to sleep, thinking about the dress in the closet. That was at the end of August.

In the fall, my husband and I invited Maria to meet a member of our church whose wife had died of cancer. Pedro had attended our church for more than ten years, but he and Maria had never met. Together with other pastors, we organized a blind date and arranged for Maria to be seated next to Pedro at a "Night of Hope with Joel and Victoria Osteen" in the Miami arena.

Pedro and Maria fell in love. Months later, we stood on a dock as Maria walked down the aisle in her off-white wedding dress. My husband performed an elegant ceremony, and we had an amazing luncheon with family and friends. Then, after a celebration of new beginnings, Pedro and Maria bid their wedding guests farewell as they departed for their Jamaican honeymoon in their boat. Today, she wears the designer wedding ring, lives in a high-rise condominium on the beach, and she and Pedro lead young couples in premarriage counseling, create incredible makeup for our theatrical productions, and socialize with hundreds of their wonderful friends right here at church.

Does it sound too good to be true? It's 100 percent true—every word! And it's true for you my friend. Missional living, reframed with powerful positive belief in a new reality and connected to serving others while engaging in your call from God provides a renewed future . . . better than even Maria could have imagined (Eph. 3:20, TLB)!

SERVING FROM THE HEART

Sometimes leadership is refusing to accept a resignation. Whatever service you provide, consider the interests of those you lead and serve. Caring for their interests and needs isn't a matter of pandering or pampering whiny followers. Jesus served best at times by saying no to some who wanted to follow Him (as with the Gerasene demoniac), by denying the requests of others (James and John in Mark 10:35–40), and even by "firing" some whose mission wasn't in line with His (Luke 14:25–35; John 6:66). You must allow Jesus to define your servant leadership.

You will uncover your destiny by walking joyfully and obediently in God's purpose for your life. Psalm 139:16 says that before you were formed, God had already purposed all the days of your life. He knew, approved, and chose you to accomplish a specific task. He also gave you talent and abilities uniquely designed to fit into His plan and to propel you toward purposeful and abundant living.

Self-awareness is vital in discovering your God-given strengths. Barriers that keep you from stepping into your spiritual leadership journey are clear and will continue to block you unless you identify new strategies to overcome them. Servant leadership is your personal path to greater happiness and fulfillment during your life on earth, and it builds an offering of service to lay at Jesus' feet when you arrive in heaven.

God wants to use you in the lives of people. The ultimate leaders are willing to develop people to the point they eventually surpass the leaders in knowledge, ability, and even position. Although many Christian leaders like to be seen as servant leaders, few want to be treated as servants. For this reason, servanthood must come from the heart.

As women leaders, we are called to lead in different arenas—in our homes, on our jobs, and in our ministries. In Christian service and ministry, the only acceptable style and attitude of leadership is that of servant leadership. Any style of leadership that isn't like Jesus Christ can't be called Christian. There's no room for selfish leadership, ruler leadership, or self-serving leadership for believers. We must never move from servant leadership to some other style of leadership.

THINGS TO CONSIDER:

1. How do you intentionally function as a servant leader in your leadership role?

    Putting the needs of others before my own, especially MSF gals

2. What aspects of your leadership could not be classified as servant leadership?

    Wanting more prestige/wanting to be noticed.

3. Find a quiet place, spend a few moments in prayer asking for guidance, and write your vision for your life and ministry.

    To - make disciples
    - build character + skills in others
    - coach myself + others into fulness of life
    - rely on God

4. What barriers are keeping you from stepping into your spiritual leadership journey?

    - insecurities
    - not trusting God, so not listening to Him

5. What new strategies can you develop to overcome them? Describe one strategy here.

    - Spend more time listening to the Lord, then obeying.

CHAPTER TWELVE

COACHING: CREATING A CONTAGIOUS CULTURE

Self-pity is our worst enemy and if we yield to it, we can never do anything wise in the world.

—HELEN ADAMS KELLER

Leading others is really about leading yourself. How can you model the characteristics you desire to see in those who follow you? You don't get in life what you *want*, you get what you *are*. You can serve people without loving them, but you can't love people without serving them.

Jesus understood His identity. He understood that all things had been given to Him by the Father. There was nothing people could give Him that the Father had not already given Him. Many leaders are too insecure to serve because they fear losing the esteem of those they serve. The Lord knew where He had come from and where He was going. What is your vision for where you are going in your ministry? In your family? In your own future?

LEADERSHIP SELF-DEVELOPMENT PLAN

The real question you need to answer is: How can I change so others can follow me? Prepare a three-month self-development plan that includes:

1. A personal vision statement
2. A personal values statement

Living a life of faith under the guidance of the Holy Spirit is an expectation of every believer. Christians live the balance of life on earth while actively pursuing a life led by the Spirit, but spiritual growth for greater leadership capacity requires action on your part.

Spiritual growth doesn't just happen; it requires a great deal of effort. This doesn't mean you do it all on your own, or that God does it all. Spiritual growth is a collaborative effort between you and God. Take time to write your leadership self-development plan now.

COACHING QUESTIONS: SERVANT LEADERSHIP

1. Ask yourself, "Would subordinates hire me to lead them? Right now would my team or leaders say, 'We want you to serve us best by leading us?'"
2. What evidence do you have to prove that those under your leadership feel valued and esteemed?
3. How do you honor your team's contributions?
4. What do you do to recognize and appreciate others' work?
5. How can you assess if you are using people to accomplish your goals, instead of working together to accomplish God's goals?
6. How are your team members becoming servant leaders as a result of your servant leadership?
7. What are you doing to develop those under you? Are they reaching their potential? Are they learning? Serving? Growing? Are you building leaders or followers?
8. Who could replace you tomorrow?
9. What ways can you assess if you and your team are accomplishing organizational goals?
10. How are you sharing the credit and regularly saying thanks to others?
11. How can you increase unity with your coworkers? With your family?

POSITIVE POWER PRAYER:
COACHING FROM THE INSIDE OUT

God's power of connecting is already at work in your life, but to increase your awareness of the Holy Spirit in your life, it's important that you base your intention and focus your attention on God's Word. Focused attention is like a muscle you can strengthen through exercise. Begin with a prayer of thanksgiving; be grateful for where you are in your life today. Read one Scripture out loud and insert your first name into the sentence.

As you speak the Scripture, declare the promise and reframe your circumstances into a positive outcome with a hopeful future. Stop. Now, do it again. Your faith is created as you envision yourself living in your amazing future. As you are connecting, God is making things happen for you that you are making happen for others. As you think through your personal process of connecting, focus on these Scriptures and speak to your future:

- May the Lord make your love [_____] for each other and for everyone else grow by leaps and bounds. (1 Thess. 3:12, CEV)
- Be kind and loving to each other [_____], and forgive each other just as God forgave you in Christ. (Eph. 4:32, NCV)
- "Treat people in the same way that you want them to treat you. If you [_____] love those who love you, why should you be commended? Even sinners love those who love them. If you [_____] do good to those who do good to you, why should you be commended? Even sinners do that. If you [_____] lend to those from whom you expect repayment, why should you be commended? Even sinners lend to sinners expecting to be paid back in full. Instead, love your enemies, do good, and lend expecting nothing in return. If you do, you [_____] will have a great reward. You will be acting the way children of the Most High act, for he is kind to ungrateful and wicked people." (Luke 6:31–35, CEB)
- [_____] Show respect for everyone. Love Christians everywhere. Fear God and honor the government. (1 Peter 2:17, TLB)

- But the fruit of the Spirit [the result of His presence within us [_____]] is love [unselfish concern for others], joy, [inner] peace, patience [not the ability to wait, but how we act while waiting], kindness, goodness, faithfulness, gentleness, self-control. Against such things there is no law. (Gal. 5:22–23, AMP)

- My dear friends, as a follower of our Lord Jesus Christ, I [_____] beg you to get along with each other. Don't take sides. Always try to agree in what you think. (1 Cor. 1:10, CEV)

- Give a warm welcome to any brother who wants to join you [_____], even though his faith is weak. Don't criticize him for having different ideas from yours about what is right and wrong. (Rom. 14:1, TLB)

- But if we [_____] are living in the light of God's presence, just as Christ does, then we have wonderful fellowship and joy with each other, and the blood of Jesus his Son cleanses us from every sin. (1 John 1:7, TLB)

- [_____] But the wisdom that comes from heaven is first of all pure and full of quiet gentleness. Then it is peace-loving and courteous. It allows discussion and is willing to yield to others; it is full of mercy and good deeds. It is wholehearted and straightforward and sincere. (James 3:17, TLB)

- [_____] By our purity, knowledge, patience, and kindness we have shown ourselves to be God's servants—by the Holy Spirit, by our true love. (2 Cor. 6:6, GNT)

- How wonderful it is [_____], how pleasant, for God's people to live together in harmony! (Ps. 133:1, GNT)

- "It is also true that we [_____] must love God with all our heart, mind, and strength, and that we must love others as much as we love ourselves. These commandments are more important than all the sacrifices and offerings that we could possibly make." (Mark 12:33, CEV)

- Encourage each other every day while you [_____] have the opportunity. If you do this, none of you will be deceived by sin and become stubborn. (Heb. 3:13, GW)

- [_____] My dear friends, we must love each other. Love comes from God, and when we love each other, it shows that we have been given new life. We are now God's children, and we know him. (1 John 4:7, CEV)
- "'So love the Lord your God [_____] with all your heart, with all your soul, with all your mind, and with all your strength. The second most important commandment is this: 'Love your neighbor as you love yourself.' No other commandment is greater than these." (Mark 12:30–31, GW)
- So [_____] let's strive for the things that bring peace and the things that build each other up. (Rom. 14:19, CEB)
- Let us [_____] not become proud in ways in which we should not. We must not make hard feelings among ourselves as Christians or make anyone jealous. (Gal. 5:26, NLV)
- We [_____] know what real love is because Jesus gave up his life for us. So we also ought to give up our lives for our brothers and sisters. (1 John 3:16, NLT)
- [_____] Just as iron sharpens iron, friends sharpen the minds of each other. (Prov. 27:17, CEV)
- Do your best to improve your faith. You [_____] can do this by adding goodness, understanding, self-control, patience, devotion to God, concern for others, and love. (2 Peter 1:5–7, CEV)
- We [_____] must also consider how to encourage each other to show love and to do good things. (Heb. 10:24, GW)
- "When you [_____] are praying and you remember that you are angry with another person about something, forgive that person. Forgive them so that your Father in heaven will also forgive your sins." (Mark 11:25, ERV)
- Whenever we [_____] have the opportunity, we have to do what is good for everyone, especially for the family of believers. (Gal. 6:10, GW)
- But if we [_____] say we love God and don't love each other, we are liars. We cannot see God. So how can we love God, if we don't love the people we can see? The commandment that God has given us is:

"Love God and love each other!" (1 John 4:20–21, CEV)

- Above all [_____], have fervent and unfailing love for one another, because love covers a multitude of sins [it overlooks unkindness and unselfishly seeks the best for others]. (1 Peter 4:8, AMP)
- God is the one who makes us patient and cheerful. I pray that he will help you [_____] live at peace with each other, as you follow Christ. Then all of you together will praise God, the Father of our Lord Jesus Christ. Honor God by accepting each other, as Christ has accepted you. (Rom. 15:5–7, CEV)

PART 4

LEADERSHIP ATTRIBUTE: ENGAGING

I don't always know where this life is going. I can't see the end of the road, but here is the great part: Courage is not about knowing the path. It is about taking the first step. It is about Peter getting out of the boat, stepping out onto the water with complete faith that Jesus will not let him drown.

—KATIE J. DAVIS

ATTRIBUTE AFFIRMATION:
I GET THINGS DONE AND DELIVER RESULTS TO ACHIEVE
MY GOAL AND EXPAND MY SUCCESS.

CHAPTER THIRTEEN

ESSENTIAL ACTION: EXECUTION

Act, and God will act.

—JOAN OF ARC

Engagement, or engaging, is a process that should be transformational for you as a leader. In this process you move from being a person things happen to, to an individual who makes things happen. Servant leadership is at the core of developing engagement.

Engagement is a critical component of your leadership process. You must engage followers so they remain creative, productive, and innovative. When they're engaged, they can cope with challenges and work to achieve goals. Women leaders who recognize the importance of engaging servant leaders should be able to foster connectivity to create a community. Additionally, leaders can inspire servant leaders to creatively address challenges, enhancing the effectiveness, meaningfulness, and relevance of the church or organization within the community. Your role in building the internal engagement of the community cannot be overlooked.

LIFE ON PURPOSE

At fourteen years old, a slender, blue-eyed brunette named Marie Johnsrud sat transfixed in her seat as the preacher gave the invitation to the altar for young people who felt called into full-time ministry. The evangelist painted a dramatic picture of a world lost in spiritual darkness and hopelessness. He described foreign lands and begged for workers to sacrifice their lives to travel to these far-off continents to become missionaries.

Marie understood loss. She knew what tragedy felt like, especially for fatherless children and mothers. Her father, a young Norwegian immigrant factory worker, had suddenly died from arsenic poisoning he had ingested while working in the local smelter. There was no explanation or compensation from the company; there was only a funeral for a father of three young girls and a young, unemployed widow. Through their despair, Marie's entire family discovered the hope of Jesus Christ, and their world transformed for the better. After listening to the evangelist that evening, Marie leapt up from her chair and walked to the altar with a resolute commitment to answer the call—she would be a missionary!

Years passed as seasons of growth and development transitioned her through her young life. To answer her calling, Marie knew she needed to be trained and equipped for a life of dedicated service. She attended a business college and became skilled on the typewriter. She took piano lessons, practicing relentlessly for hours to be able to play keyboards (accordion, piano, or organ) so she could accompany a congregation for worship services. She applied herself to study and attended a Bible college in Seattle. Throughout her teenage years, Marie served diligently in the church that had been planted by her parents inside their farmhouse. Marie was a leader, and she knew it. By finding her voice through church planting, Marie was ready to launch out into the world to assume her "transformissional" leadership calling.

Marie pushed forward. Applications were filed, interviews were held, public preaching engagements had to be found, and her required funds to fulfill the missions board's designated budget had to be raised, but Marie would not be discouraged. She had heard the call. Years passed before the official letter finally arrived, confirming that she was approved to serve as a missionary for the Assemblies of God. She announced to her family and friends that she had been accepted and her assignment was for the French West African nation of Burkina Faso.

By the fall of 1945 her preparations were complete, and Marie found herself standing in the cold morning mist with her parents, sisters, extended family, and church family at the railway station in Tacoma, Washington. With tears streaming down their faces, the family prayed and sang in unity as Marie hugged and kissed her loved ones goodbye. By train, ship, and bus, Marie traveled seven thousand miles to begin her missionary ministry in the country that would be her new home for the next thirty-five years.

Upon arriving, the community of missionaries already working in Africa assigned Maria to the Bible translation team and to care for the children of the missionaries. She loved her work. Living in the bush and in the city, she flourished while adapting to the African way of life. However, it didn't come without obstacles and difficult tests to her endurance.

Translating the Bible into the Mossi language meant she needed to translate from French, not from English. Mossi is a derivative of French, and the best translation needed to be based in the French text. She worked on an old-fashioned manual typewriter. She later recounted how she prayed God would send her an electric typewriter so she could make faster progress. To her relief and amazement, an electric typewriter arrived from the United States. Her heart sank, however, when she realized she had no electricity to run the new machine! Eventually, God provided a power generator to run the typewriter, allowing her and her team to produce the first translation of the Scriptures in Mossi.

Marie has shared many stories of her missionary life of faith and miraculous provision. One night, while driving through the bush on her motorcycle, she was caught in a blinding thunderstorm. The rain and lightning were coming down with such intensity that she could barely see a few feet ahead. The jungle path was difficult to maneuver and was quickly beginning to flood. To keep going, she stared straight ahead and stayed focused on the primitive path in front of her. Suddenly, a middle-aged African man, dressed all in white, stepped from the jungle onto the edge of the path. His appearance was so sudden it caught her by surprise, so she slowed down thinking he wanted to cross in front of her. However, as she turned her head to acknowledge him he motioned, waving his arms fervently, that she was to turn off the road. Marie was shaken and confused. She turned her head back to the path and steered the motorcycle to the edge of the jungle. She didn't know what to do next, so she turned back to ask the man what he was trying to tell her, but he was gone. Vanished!

Marie was stunned. He couldn't have disappeared so quickly. Now, with even more concern, she jumped off the motorcycle and began to run in and out of the jungle foliage to find this mysterious, disappearing stranger. To her shock and amazement, as she proceeded to walk forward up the unlit jungle trail, she discovered the bridge over a deep and dangerous ravine in front of her had been washed out by the storm. Had the stranger not stopped her journey, she would have crashed over the cliff to certain death. For the rest of her life, Marie strongly believed that traveler was an angel, and that God had supernaturally protected her from tragedy that night.

When Marie completed her thirty-fifth year of service in Africa, she felt led to return home to Tacoma and her family. And so Marie settled into retirement. For her, that meant on Mondays she taught English classes to immigrants. Tuesdays she worked in the church offices doing anything she was asked. On Wednesdays she attended noon prayer meetings at the church and took care of little boys after school. Thursdays, she went to the Mission to serve food to the hungry, and on Fridays she found elderly people who needed help in countless ways. Serving others always opened the door to active living.

Years passed, and an invitation came from Africa for Marie to return to Burkina Faso for an honorary appearance to commemorate her retirement from missionary service. She was reluctant to go but her sisters, Ingie and Lorraine, insisted. Ingie and Marie traveled together to the city of Ouagadougou for the ceremony. Upon arriving, Marie was convinced they had misunderstood the event details because the building was not a church; it was stadium packed with thousands of people! When Marie was called to the platform, thousands and thousands of Africans jumped to their feet chanting, "Mother, Mama!" Although Marie had never had a husband or child of her own, nor had she ever owned a piece of property or had a bank account, she had impacted the legacy of an entire city.

Thousands of Africans testified of Marie's ministry as she served with her open home and open heart. Marie had mothered, nursed, and nurtured a broken generation. Thousands of lives were transformed through her "transformissional" leadership. One of those lives was mine. Marie Johnsrud was my mother's sister. The influence of her selfless leadership on my life cannot be measured. I constantly look to her example when I need to remember what true sacrifice looks like.

SELF-AWARENESS

Much of what has been discussed regarding ministry leadership, connectivity, and engagement encompasses efforts to build change in leadership practice. Individualism is abandoned in favor of establishing a common ground for leaders to achieve equality through service. The leader isn't exalted but is embraced as a partner in building a community of faith. Connectivity and engagement require active participation from the leader to build active participation in followers. Followers become leaders within the community. This change marks a shift in the system.

Being a servant leader doesn't mean ignoring your own needs. You must develop a sense of self-awareness in your leadership practice. This requires that you be aware of emotions and the practicalities of a situation.[1] You must also be able to understand the need for change and the role that engaging can play in making change possible. Moving forward, it's critical to recognize when engaging can be used as a foundational change in your own ministry. Understanding the process of reframing and gaining self-awareness regarding what is practical and feasible in the context of ministry leadership will be essential for making these determinations.

Self-awareness is a valuable component of your leadership. It helps you understand how emotions drive decision-making and behavior, and how to focus on changing this process to engage new perspectives on problems and issues. Self-awareness is innately related to the competency of self-clarity, which is essential to the development of effective leadership. Self-clarity provides unique and distinctive support for effective leadership. Part of self-clarity is understanding what God is telling you and being willing to accept the dreams and visions He gives you.

> Part of self-clarity is understanding what God is telling you and being willing to accept the dreams and visions He gives you.

DREAM LEADER

Dreams are part of the divine GPS that comes standard in all humans. Dreams reveal clues to the destiny God has for you. "The Hebrew word for dream is *chalom*. It means to 'make plump, to swell, to extend to it's fullness . . . to enlarge, to make fat.' It gives an image of a future that will have you 'bursting at the dreams!'"[2] Does the Holy Spirit still give visions and dreams? In Joel 2:28, Joel prophesied that the Holy Spirit would give believers visions and dreams when God poured out His Spirit on all flesh.

On the Day of Pentecost, Peter exercised the gift of prophecy, confirming Joel's promise: "Your young men will see visions, your old men will dream dreams" (Acts 2:17). The context in Joel emphasizes that the Holy Spirit will be poured out on all flesh. He will minister through sons and daughters, old and young, men and women, people of every background, every color, and every nationality. Clearly God wants every believer, from every class of society, to be involved.[3] So the answer is a resounding yes! God wants every woman leader to dream a new dream for herself and for those she influences.

Sometimes we experience dreams when we sleep, but more often we envision them in our hearts and minds, and they become a reality when we apply faith to them. All dreams begin with hope—hope for something better. Hope demands that you see the invisible and have the stubborn capacity to believe the impossible and expect the intangible.

You must never let go of the hope God has placed in your heart. "It's an unbreakable spiritual lifeline, reaching past all appearances right to the very presence of God" (Heb. 6:19–20, MSG). You must never lose the thrill of dreaming, and it must stay active in your leadership. According to Scripture, your dreaming is another sign you are filled with the Holy Spirit (Joel 2; Acts 2).

However, what if you've lost the desire to dream because of disappointments? Pray for hope. Even if you're discouraged by the pain of the past, pray for hope. The Bible says no matter what is happening in your life, you have God's authority to claim hope in every situation. "When everything was hopeless, Abraham believed anyway, deciding to live not on the basis of what he saw he *couldn't* do but on what God said he *would* do" (Rom. 4:18, MSG, italics in original). Sometimes, all you can do is hang on to hope and believe for your dream.

Hope stimulates the dream, but faith activates us to move. Faith engages us to take ownership of what we dream. Faith writes out the vision and insists we execute the contract. "Now faith is the assurance (title deed, confirmation) of things hoped for (divinely guaranteed), and the evidence of things not seen [the conviction of their reality—faith comprehends as fact what cannot be experienced by the physical senses]" (Heb. 11:1, AMP). Faith calls what is not yet as though it is!

Dreaming is an essential trait for effective women leaders, but you must commit to the vision 100 percent. A dream written down becomes a goal. A goal executed with a plan leads to success; however, total commitment is required to keep the plan on course. If your dreams are dead, what excuse have you been telling yourself? In other words, what "bull-oney" have you been believing?

Bullfighting is a fascinating sport. I had expected some kind of "slaughter house" décor, but the bullfighting ring in Mexico City was more like the many football stadiums I had attended all my life. Although it seemed inexplicable to me why millions would rate bullfighting as an important sport, my husband and I reluctantly agreed to accompany friends to see the phenomenon for ourselves.

As it turns out, bullfighting is a series of small commitments that are completely meaningless until the bullfighter makes a big commitment. The female bullfighter I saw that night was incredible. She was artistic, stylish, athletic, and courageous. However, until she climbed over the safety fence and put herself in front of the bull, everything else was pointless.

Getting your classes finished, acquiring your license, telling your family you're called by God to serve are all good choices. However, until you climb over the safety fence of excuses to face the Enemy of your soul, nothing you've done to engage with your mission will matter.

Commit to your dream today! Goals are dreams with deadlines. Dreams, when written down, become goals. "People who regularly write down their goals earn nine times as much over their lifetimes as the people who do not. However, 80 percent of Americans say they don't have goals. Additionally, there is another 16 percent of Americans who say they do have goals, but they don't write them down. Fewer than 4 percent of Americans write down their goals, and fewer than 1 percent actually review them regularly."[4]

Be specific. When you sit down in your favorite restaurant and review the menu, you don't turn to the waitperson and say, "Just bring me whatever you have!" You spend time reviewing the many choices, ask lots of questions regarding the ingredients and how they are prepared, and then you select your personal choice. That's exactly how you must handle your personal goals for life. Be specific. The clearer and more vividly you visualize a goal, the easier it becomes to achieve or acquire it. If possible, envision yourself accomplishing the goal. Role-play yourself doing it. Close your eyes and imagine how it feels to realize that goal.

DETERMINED

Strong determination is required to achieve a goal or realize a vision, a conviction, even a passion. Determination presses forward in spite of resistance or obstacles . . . especially when those obstacles come in the form of loss.

It was a beautiful sunny day as I dragged myself into the Lutheran convalescent hospital in Tacoma, Washington. My hero, my eighty-six-year-old dad, was struggling to breathe as he fought a losing battle with congestive heart failure. As a successful pastor in one church for fifty consecutive years, my father had a lifetime of evidence to prove to me what it means to be determined. Realizing dad was close to passing from earth into heaven, my cousin Suzanne stepped up and asked him, "Uncle

Fulton, what one thing can you tell us about life that we need to remember?" From his bed and with great effort my dad carefully articulated in a strong husky whisper, "Never, ever, ever give up!" After thousands of sermons, after thousands of funerals delivered at gravesides, after thousands of weddings, and after thousands and thousands of counseling sessions, the last words of admonition my dying father spoke to his children were: "Never give up!"

When I'm discouraged, exhausted, and tempted to give up, I hear Dad's encouragement

> The clearer and more vividly you visualize a goal, the easier it becomes to achieve or acquire it.

in my heart. Today, because of my parent's lifestyle examples, determination is a core value of who I am. Staying determined to finish the course turns out to be a key to all success.

During WWII, in the midst of the horrible Battle of Britain, Winston Churchill addressed the young students at Harrow School. There, he gave his famous exhortation, "Never give in. Never give in. Never, never, never—in nothing, great or small, large or petty—never give in, except to convictions of honor and good sense." When it comes to determination and persistence, many people fall on the extreme edges of the spectrum. On the one end is the defeatist attitude: *Why me? Who am I to do this? I'm not equipped. The things and people who oppose me are stronger and smarter than I am. It's too hard. I can't take any more failure. I'm tired.*

On the other end is unshakable determination. A leader can find herself stuck in naïve stubbornness. Sometimes women can't give in because they aren't willing to admit they might have been wrong. Some of us are so analytical that to do it any other way would be ludicrous. *Why would I do something I know is stupid?* Notice something similar in the extremes? The emphasis is on me. When the "me needs" of the leader override the needs of those the leader serves, the leader and the team aren't functioning in a healthy manner.

In the center of the extremes is where determination and persistence become essential and usable traits of a leader—keeping a balanced pressure on the interface of an issue, pressing forward in spite of resistance or obstacles. Many times, the biggest obstacle or resistance is simply getting "self" out of the way.

ESSENTIAL ACTION: EXECUTION

THINGS TO CONSIDER:

1. Do you feel you are living a "life on purpose"? What does that look like to you?

   - Yes-ish. I live to serve + reach the lost, and to disciple the found.

2. Describe one dream you have in your heart and mind that can become a reality with God's help.

   - Loving people well.
   - But I need to learn how to love myself well.

3. Create a goal right now to fulfill that dream! Be specific and list the steps you need to take to accomplish your dream.

   - Learn to love who God made me to be
   - Be open with my time/resources
   - Intentionally plan life
   - Intentionally invite people into relationship
   - Don't stop or give up.

4. Now create a timeline for those steps. When will you start, when will you finish, how long should each step take?

   - 1 month to love myself
   - Jan: evaluate time / who
   - Feb: plan + invite

5. Take a moment to pray about your dream and the goals you have set to see that dream come true. Listen for God's guidance and change anything in your previous answers that you feel He is leading you to change.

CHAPTER FOURTEEN

GETTING THINGS DONE

If we are to better the future we must disturb the present.

—CATHERINE BOOTH

Self-clarity is being aware of personality, and how one is perceived by others. The achievement of self-clarity represents a deeply personal journey that leads to better leadership practice. Self-clarity can precipitate identity development, a process that serves as the basis for building authenticity and genuineness in your behavior and actions.

You must be yourself.[1] You don't have to prove your specific attributes to others. Take solace in the fact that God made each person unique. As a result, you must stop trying to be like everyone else and develop your own identity.[2] However, you can only establish a unique identity if you achieve self-clarity and acquire a unique identity you can personally own.

The journey toward self-clarity and the achievement of a unique identity challenges you to connect your inner self to the external world. This process requires reflection and insight, which can bring about "a growing perception of an inter-relatedness of everything and a striving towards wholeness."[3] Self-clarity and identity development focus on the development of an integrated whole in which your strengths and vulnerabilities are acknowledged and recognized as important elements of who you are.

Creating a pathway to self-clarity will typically involve conflict as you attempt to come to terms with weaknesses and work to integrate all aspects of yourself to create an accepting, complete identity. This process will require you to come to terms with a number of personal issues. However, the journey is supported through Scripture. Matthew 7:1–6 provides a starting point for understanding your need to engage in this process. Evangelist D. L. Moody was once asked which people gave him the most trouble. His response was, "I've had more trouble with Dwight L. Moody than any other man alive." It's been said that a man is not defeated by his opponents but by himself. Finding a pathway to self-clarity is a challenging process that is tied to the development of emotional intelligence (EI). This includes your ability to manage your feelings and impulses while motivating others, demonstrating empathy, and retaining connection through optimism and energy. Positive thinking and the ability to understand relationships and how others view you are also critical elements of effective EI.

Self-clarity can provide the insight you need to acquire EI and to utilize this foundation for meeting the needs of your followers. It also involves your ability to shape the perceptions of others. A concrete pathway to self-clarity involves introspection, reflection, and efforts to integrate the whole to reveal one's true identity. Efforts to utilize this identity in practice will provide you with the ability to engage *authentically* and *genuinely* to build important relationships with others.

This is a personal journey that you must undertake to build effective leadership. Although this aspect of leadership practice is essential for providing guidance for others, your development of self-clarity, identity, self-awareness, and EI is not the end of the journey. You must also work to lead others to self-clarity. You are charged with the responsibility of leading followers to live Christ-centered lives. In this process, you must help them cross boundaries that may limit them in their ability to achieve personal growth, achieve self-sacrifice, and recognize the plight of others in society. As a leader, you can change the behaviors of a follower if you modify the follower's identity to help that person overcome the negative elements of self-concept that drive their behavior. You can influence self-concept and self-clarity to change behavior!

At the core of building leadership competencies is the use of servant leadership to help develop the essential attributes needed to build effective leadership. In the context of self-clarity, servant leadership can help you develop a fundamental understanding of your role. Can you see the dynamic interplay between connectivity, engagement, reframing, and self-clarity?

The pathway to self-clarity requires the development of a unique identity. This identity must be expressed through your ability to find your own voice. When you achieve this outcome, you will be able to inspire and help others accomplish similar results in their lives. Finding your voice is an important component of living a life dedicated to Christ!

> As a leader, you can change the behaviors of a follower if you modify the follower's identity to help that person overcome the negative elements of self-concept that drive their behavior.

FINDING MY VOICE AS A LEADER

He was a white, chubby, middle-aged Caucasian pastor with thinning hair and shiny skin. He leaned in so close I could feel his breath, and then asked again in a louder, more incredulous tone, "You mean *you* are the pastor? *You* preach? *You* attend board meetings? *You?*"

Seated next to me inside our classroom, this prominent denominational leader was also attending seminary as a fellow graduate student. Through classroom conversation, it had suddenly occurred to him that my leadership role in our church was unlike the women in his congregation. He was staring at me with eyes wide-open in total shock. My personification of a woman leader wasn't what he expected, and he didn't approve. In his opinion, I was outside the boundaries of acceptability.

Every believer is a leader. Not just men. Finding my voice as a woman pastor serving in an urban community has been a long journey. For many years I was confused by conflicting theological understandings of a woman's place in God's economy. Professional pursuits, being a wife, motherhood, and education seemed to collide into an unmanageable, unsolvable combustion of chaos. To me, it seemed that potlucks, coffees, endless conversations around recipes and fashion, along with gossip sessions seemed to dominate the landscape of women's ministries. However, when I began to do life with women of our Miami church community who were struggling to juggle work, childcare, and extended family responsibilities with little or no support, I woke up fast to the crisis.

Peter wrote that all followers of Christ have been made royalty so we can declare the praise of God, which is the work of a prophet. The Holy Spirit equips every believer as a prophet to bring the truth, as a priest to serve compassionately, and as member of the royal family, calling others into the accountability of love. Though pastors and teachers are distinctly called to build up the body into spiritual maturity (Eph. 4:11–13), every Christian is called to build up the body into maturity by "speaking the truth in love" (Eph. 4:15). The royalty of every believer also means every believer has the authority to fight and defeat the world, the flesh, and the Devil (Eph. 6:11–18; James 4:7; 1 John 2:27; 4:4; 5:4).

Women are in crisis. Now is the time when women must step up and take a new kind of responsibility for their dreams, purposes, and calling. God has equipped us with the personal capacities for change, but the crisis for women continues to grow. Most often, young women lack support and encouragement to believe they can achieve their callings. Here are the facts: less than half of American kids under the age of eighteen live in a home with two married parents. Fifty-four percent of families in this country are nontraditional.[4] Households headed by a female make up the poorest demographic in America.[5] Of the single mothers, nearly two-thirds are working in low-wage retail, service, or administrative jobs with limited economic future.[6] All of this is happening while women outnumber men at every level of higher education.[7] In 2014, women working full time, year round were paid only seventy-nine cents for every dollar paid to their male counterparts.[8]

Leadership is influence, and every woman influences someone.[9] She influences her family, her coworkers, her church, and her community. I found my voice to ministry leadership by rising to God's calling to encourage women to lead. As defined through the leadership competencies identified, finding one's voice is the process of discovering and confidently articulating individual values, convictions, and calling with authenticity in your unique and personal style.

Much like achieving self-clarity, finding one's voice is a journey. Scholars who have examined this process in ministry leadership acknowledge this reality: "Every leader is created differently, and each brings his or her unique style to the tasks of leadership."[10] As a result, "Leaders need to discover how they lead most effectively, and then lean into that leadership strength while adding other skills and aptitudes along the way."[11] Finding one's voice is a critical theme in Scripture, as Isaiah 58:1 encourages individuals to find and use their voice: "Shout it aloud, do not hold back. Raise your voice like a trumpet."

Meaning is a critical component of creating effective leadership. Leaders who find meaning "convey energy and enthusiasm because the goal is important to them personally, because they are actively enjoying its pursuit, and because their work plays to their strengths."[12] Finding your voice helps you to create a foundation of passion and joy, both of which are integral to being a connective and engaging leader. To bring your voice to life, you must align your capabilities as a leader and the activities you use to achieve effective leadership. Finding your voice becomes a lived experience; one shared with all followers.

Developing confidence in your voice can be challenging. A lack of confidence often stems from the overwhelming anxiety that your voice isn't adequate or acceptable for others. Remember to "Cast all your anxiety on him because he cares for you" (1 Peter 5:7). You can become so focused on yourself and your anxiety over how others will perceive you that you fail to lead. Achieving self-clarity, developing an identity, and finding your true voice should produce the confidence you need to be an effective leader.

In his letter to the Romans, Paul wrote: "I long to see you so that I may impart to you some spiritual gift to make you strong—that is, that you and I may be mutually encouraged by each other's faith" (Rom. 1:11–12). In many ways, you are the inheritor of Paul's mission as commanded by Christ: to spread the gospel and lead others into the kingdom of heaven. Yet since "many are invited, but few are chosen," women leaders often struggle to find the right combination of traits that will allow them to become effective leaders (Matt. 22:14). Understanding servant leadership is the key for leaders to serve their flock, understand themselves better, and spread the good news.

With understanding comes wisdom. Only when you understand your own strengths and weaknesses can you recognize how to be authentic. Peter feared he was incapable of leading, and when he denied the Lord he was ashamed. Yet this human weakness didn't prevent him from gaining the courage, through the gift of the Holy Spirit, to become a formidable leader in the early church.

KNOW WHAT YOU STAND FOR

Through the process of finding meaning, you will come to know yourself. With the example of Christ and the teachings of the church, servant leadership allows you to cultivate these traits and incorporate them. True leadership isn't found in a book but through cultivating servant leadership, following the example of Christ, and relying on the guidance of the Holy Spirit. This is how you find joy in leading others to Christ.

Highly effective women in ministry know what they stand for. It's as simple as that. Self-knowledge creates a level of self-confidence that is both formidable and engaging. Anchored leaders articulate how their values affect their professional and private lives, and they talk about their values in ways that convince others. Highly effective women leaders not only have deep beliefs, they encourage others to have them as well.

LEADING IN SPITE OF LIFE

To hear the doorbell ring so early on a Saturday morning was sort of weird. The July sun was shining as Ella looked out her second-floor bedroom window to see who was at the front door. She couldn't believe her eyes; it was her friend Sheriff James banging hard to get a response. His county squad car was parked in her driveway, and the back passenger door was standing open. Dressed in full uniform, with his handcuffs twirling, the aggressive young sheriff was pushing hard to make the front door open. Before she could get down the stairs to answer the door, she heard her husband loudly greet the sheriff. "Yeah, yeah. Quit banging so hard. I'm coming outside. Yes, I'm here. Not so hard, you don't have to do that! I'm cooperating!"

Ella ran to follow as her husband stormed out the door, across the porch to the side of the police car. James commanded her husband, David, to, "Assume the position against the back of my car, so I can pat you down. Anything sharp in your pockets?

> Only when you understand your own strengths and weaknesses can you recognize how to be authentic.

I have to read you your rights. Sorry Ella, but David is under arrest!" Everything was a blur. She couldn't breathe. Her two kids had heard all the commotion and were standing, terrified, on the porch, watching as their dad was put into handcuffs.

"Ella, there's nothing I can say or do about this. I can't express how sorry I am to be here, but when I heard they were going to arrest David, I volunteered to come! I know how awful this is for you and the kids. I wanted to be the one to take him downtown." By now David was standing near the squad car, bent over spread-eagle, and James was patting him down. The handcuffs went on instantly, as David shook his head and cried loudly to Ella, "I'm so sorry! I'm innocent!"

David squatted down and slid into the back of the squad car. James slammed the car door shut and then turned to Ella and said slowly, "David was identified this morning by two junior high girls who were out early jogging near their home. According to their story, your husband cruised by in his truck and stopped to talk with them. He grabbed one and the other girl took off with a cell phone to call their parents. David let go of the teenager quickly, but her parents are pressing charges. I don't really know what happened, but I'm here to take him in."

Ella was in an emotional meltdown. The sheriff sensed her terror. She was trembling and shaking as her friend went on to explain. "Once we get downtown, David will be held in the jail until he sees a judge. You probably need to call him an attorney. After we get David booked in, I can call you and let you know more. I'm really sorry."

That was the last time Ella saw David for many years. As the sordid and complicated story unfolded over the coming months, making national media headlines, her husband was accused of crimes that led to a prison sentence of thirty years.

So what happened next? What did Ella do? How did she cope with the shame of her husband's trial and incarceration? What happened to her professional career and her ministry within her local church? Did Ella lose her four-bedroom home in the suburbs? Did her girls drop out of school and turn to a life of addiction and self-destruction?

Nope. As a woman leader in her church and in her professional life, Ella did what women experiencing horrific crisis are doing every day. She took one foot and placed it firmly in her future, and then she picked up her other foot and took the next step—one painful day at a time. One moment, one breath, one tear, one wakeful night, one empty family holiday, one mortgage payment, one paycheck at a time—she kept going. Her mission was her family.

She reframed her circumstances by talking to God and hearing Him say, "Ella, I'm providing you with the job of your dreams. Get up and go to work. No matter how tired you are, or how hopeless you feel, I'm with you every step of the way. You can do this!" Her connectivity was her church, her coworkers, parents of other students in her children's Christian school, and her family. She engaged her world every day, not allowing life to just happen to her. Instead, she took action to make her vision for the future happen for her kids.

In God's economy, as Ella embodied her mission for others she received healing, transformation, and energy for herself. Her servant leadership ministry, her acts of service performed for her family, her church, and her organization became the process of a miraculous transformation for her life. She didn't die; she lived. She thrived!

Today, Ella drives a brand-new car. Her daughter attends an outstanding private Christian university. She's the grandmother of a darling preschooler. Her children are flourishing. She lives in the same house, vacations wherever she desires, loves to laugh, and enjoys an enormous circle of friends. When asking Ella about the devastation resulting from her husband's choices and the impact on her life she answers, "Actually, I don't know how I did it. Somehow, through every heartbreak, God made a way. We never missed a meal; my kids have had everything they needed. My career continues to pay me well. My life is full, and I know my future is going to be amazing. What the Devil meant for bad, God meant for good."

Leadership always makes the difference—every time, everywhere, for everyone. Friend, all five of the essential attributes of leadership for women are already active in your leadership. God wants to help you expand those leadership skills to transform you as you press forward to accomplish the calling on your life.

We all understand how helping others succeed is more important than winning a victory for ourselves. What we do matters less than who we are. How we do things matters less than the person we do them for. The power to connect, engage, and reframe while retaining self-clarity and using your personal voice is vital for effective leadership.

THINGS TO CONSIDER:

1. Being yourself is vital to becoming the leader you are meant to be. Briefly write about one area of your life where you feel you are not fully being yourself.

   -At home w/ Joe — I subdue who I am

2. How would you rate your ability to manage your feelings and impulses on a scale of one to ten?

   7 — More like an 8 at work, 6 at home

3. What steps do you need to take to increase your emotional intelligence to increase your rating?

   - Self-control of emotions e reframing how I think of myself.

4. You have a voice and it is a valuable tool in your leadership. Think about the women leaders in your life whom you look up to. How do they use their voices to create change?

   - Speak wisdom, encouragement, ask good questions.

5. How can you use your personal voice to connect, engage, and reframe in your leadership role?

   - I first need to be confident in my voice.

CHAPTER FIFTEEN

COACHING: PRACTICING THE DISCIPLINE OF PRODUCTIVITY

Blessed is the one who perseveres under trial because, having stood the test, that person will receive the crown of life that the Lord has promised to those who love him.

—JAMES 1:12

The dominate thought in a determined leader is, *Why am I doing this?* The need for determination may be a defense posture—dealing with opposing views from others and knowing you must stand your ground. Alternatively, it may be an offense position—holding true to your values and pressing through hard times and battling discouragement.

Where do you fall on the scale? Do you lean more toward a defeatist attitude or are you on the stubborn end of the spectrum? Are you impetuous, circumspect, or nonresponsive? To help keep focus, ask yourself these questions:

1. *What's the point?* Remind yourself why you are hanging in there when resistance or discouragement set in. When a leader is vision focused, the reason for perseverance isn't about self. Remind others why it's important to persevere in the face of opposition and difficulty.
2. *What will happen if I give in or give up?* If the reason for pressing in and pushing on isn't about you, what's the worst-case scenario if you give up? What could happen if you gave in . . . just a little?

Discouragement comes to all. Depression issues and fatigue aren't as significant when you have a clear view of what it looks like if you give up. Sometimes it's catastrophic, and like Churchill, you just can't succumb to Hitler. At other times, you have to remember life isn't a football metaphor. You don't have to win every game. What will you gain by taking your foot off the accelerator? What will happen if you stop digging in so hard? Leaders aren't cowards, and they aren't quitters. However, stepping back for a bit may bring you closer to the big vision/mission win.

3. *What does my "opposition" need?* How can you include this in your strategy? Remember, in most cases, others aren't your enemies—Satan is. Don't demonize people. Don't personalize your opposition unless the opposition is you. Personalizing, finding fault, criticizing, and complaining suck up energy and focus and obscure your path to real solutions. If your opposition is your fear, procrastination, or lack of resolve, what do you need to buck up?

4. *Am I staying determined because this is important for me?* Is your focus on you or the mission? If it's only about you, then your determination might be selfish stubbornness. Putting your team's mission first will always lead to the highest rewards for everyone.

These questions will help you keep your focus, but make sure you don't become so focused that you lose sight of your vision. Balance your determination with patience. An unmanaged driving conviction can result in impulsive acts. King Saul lost his kingdom to a shepherd boy because he refused to back off the throttle and wait on God. A rash countenance is an unwillingness to hold on, to loosen the determined grip in spite of signals to the contrary.

There's an old African story of how to trap a monkey. The trapper drops a banana inside a narrow-necked jar. When a hungry monkey sticks its arm into the tiny opening, it grabs the luscious banana. Even though it hears the trapper approaching to capture it, the greedy monkey cannot bring itself to let go of the banana. With frantic desperation, the chimp tries to pull the banana through the narrow top of the jar, but its clenched fist is too large to come out the top. This simple monkey-catching trap has been used for centuries.

There's a dynamic balance between the two extremes of being either impetuous or nonresponsive. *Circumspect*—careful to consider all circumstances and possible consequences—is the best word to describe the leader's sweet spot of holy determination.

Determination is an intention to do something. As a leader, encourage others with these words: "I can do all this through him who gives me strength" (Phil. 4:13). Your source of strength is found in the power of the Holy Spirit, and reminding yourself about this is the first step to appropriate your supernatural source.

COACHING QUESTIONS: ENGAGING

1. What is the purpose of what you do?
2. What type of impact do you want your leadership to have?
3. How does your leadership contribute to others and the world?
4. How is your leadership going to contribute to the betterment of others and your mission?
5. What parts of your ministry do you like the most? The least?
6. If you knew you were going to be in your current ministry context for the rest of your life, what would you do now to make the most of it?
7. What would your ministry team (employees or volunteers) be surprised to know about you?
8. What percentage of the authentic "you" shows through in your ministry?
9. If you achieved your ministry goals, what would be the biggest impact?
10. If you knew you couldn't fail, what would you try right now?
11. What are you working on that is making a profound difference for you and others?

12. What three goals do you want to achieve within the next three months?
13. What do you want most from your current ministry leadership role?
14. On a scale of 1 to 10, how motivated are you in your ministry/personal life? What motivates you?
15. How have your personal goals supported your ministry goals?
16. What is one step you can take today to move closer to your ministry leadership goals?
17. Describe a moment when you felt the most alive.
18. What makes you feel alive?
19. What motivates you? How do you motivate yourself?
20. What is the one thing that never fails to move you to action?

POSITIVE POWER PRAYER:
COACHING FROM THE INSIDE OUT

By *engaging*, you make an intentional effort to be the best leader you can be. The Scriptures that follow will help you increase your ability to engage. *Focused attention* is very much like a muscle that can be strengthened through exercise. Begin with a prayer of thanksgiving. *Be grateful* for where you are in your life today. Read one Scripture out loud and insert your first name into the sentence. As you speak the Scripture, declare the promise and reframe your circumstances into a positive outcome with a hopeful future. Stop. Now, do it again. Your faith is created as you envision yourself living in your amazing future. As you are engaging, God is making things happen for you that you are making happen for others. As you think through your personal process of engaging, focus on these Scriptures and speak to your future:

• Christ gives me [_____] the strength to face anything. (Phil. 4:13, CEV)

- Therefore [_____], my beloved brothers and sisters, be steadfast, immovable, always excelling in the work of the Lord [always doing your best and doing more than is needed], being continually aware that your labor [even to the point of exhaustion] in the Lord is not futile nor wasted [it is never without purpose]. (1 Cor. 15:58, AMP)

- Show yourself in all respects [_____] to be a model of good works, and in your teaching show integrity, dignity, and sound speech that cannot be condemned, so that an opponent may be put to shame, having nothing evil to say about us. (Titus 2:7–8, ESV)

- In everything we [_____] have won more than a victory because of Christ who loves us. (Rom. 8:37, CEV)

- "I tell you the truth. The person [_____] who believes in me will do the big work that I do. And he will do even bigger work because I go to my Father." (John 14:12, WE)

- [_____] Let the kindness of the Lord our God be with us. Make us successful in everything we do. Yes, make us successful in everything we do. (Ps. 90:17, GW)

- Last of all I want to remind you [_____] that your strength must come from the Lord's mighty power within you. (Eph. 6:10, TLB)

- Commit your actions to the LORD [_____], and your plans will succeed. (Prov. 16:3, NLT)

- Do your best to present yourself [_____] to God as a tried-and-true worker who isn't ashamed to teach the word of truth correctly. (2 Tim. 2:15, GW)

- I [_____] run toward the goal, so that I can win the prize of being called to heaven. This is the prize that God offers because of what Christ Jesus has done. (Phil. 3:14, CEV)

- "Ask [_____], and you will be given what you ask for. Seek, and you will find. Knock, and the door will be opened. For everyone who asks, receives. Anyone who seeks, finds. If only you [_____] will knock, the door will opened." (Matt. 7:7–8, TLB)

- [_____] Hard work is worthwhile, but empty talk will make you poor. (Prov. 14:23, CEV)

SHATTERING THE STAINED GLASS CEILING

- "I [_____] glorified you on earth by completing the work you gave me to do." (John 17:4, NET)
- Do your work with enthusiasm [_____]. Work as if you were serving the Lord, not as if you were serving only men and women. Remember that the Lord will give a reward to everyone, slave or free, for doing good. (Eph. 6:7–8, NCV)
- [_____] He who plants and he who waters are one [in importance and esteem, working toward the same purpose]; but each will receive his own reward according to his own labor. For we [_____] are God's fellow workers [His servants working together]; you are God's cultivated field [His garden, His vineyard], God's building. (1 Cor. 3:8–9, AMP)
- "I know what you [_____] have done—how hard you have worked and how you have endured." (Rev. 2:2, GW)
- Work hard [_____] and become a leader; be lazy and never succeed. (Prov. 12:24, TLB)
- God in his kindness gave each of us different gifts. If your gift [_____] is speaking what God has revealed, make sure what you say agrees with the Christian faith. If your gift is serving, then devote yourself to serving. If it is teaching, devote yourself to teaching. If it is encouraging others, devote yourself to giving encouragement. If it is sharing, be generous. If it is leadership, lead enthusiastically. If it is helping people in need, help them cheerfully. (Rom. 12:6–8, GW)
- Whatever you do [_____], whether in speech or action, do it all in the name of the Lord Jesus and give thanks to God the Father through him. (Col. 3:17, CEB)
- "In the same way, [_____] let your light shine before others, so that they may see your good works and give glory to your Father who is in heaven." (Matt. 5:16, ESV)
- "Truly I tell you [_____], whatever you bind on earth will be bound in heaven, and whatever you loose on earth will be loosed in heaven." (Matt. 18:18)
- "But as for you [_____], be strong and do not give up, for your

work will be rewarded." (2 Chron. 15:7)

- So I have seen that nothing is better [_____] than that man should be happy in his work, for that is all he can do. (Eccl. 3:22, NLV)
- Not that we are competent in ourselves to claim anything for ourselves, but our competence [_____] comes from God. (2 Cor. 3:5)
- For God is not unjust so as to forget your work [_____] and the love which you have shown for His name in ministering to [the needs of] the saints (God's people), as you do. (Heb. 6:10, AMP)
- "But more than anything else [_____], put God's work first and do what he wants. Then the other things will be yours as well." (Matt. 6:33, CEV)
- Therefore [_____], since we have this ministry, just as we received mercy [from God, granting us salvation, opportunities, and blessings], we do not get discouraged nor lose our motivation. (2 Cor. 4:1, AMP)
- So [_____], dear brothers and sisters, work hard to prove that you really are among those God has called and chosen. Do these things, and you will never fall away. (2 Peter 1:10, NLT)
- For God has not given us [_____] a spirit of fear and timidity, but of power, love, and self-discipline. (2 Tim. 1:7, NLT)
- Take care how you live [_____]. Do not live like people who are not wise, but live like people who are wise. Make good use of time because people live in very wrong ways these days. So then, be wise and understand what the Lord wants. (Eph. 5:15–17, WE)
- [_____] Every Scripture passage is inspired by God. All of them are useful for teaching, pointing out errors, correcting people, and training them for a life that has God's approval. They equip God's servants so that they are completely prepared to do good things. (2 Tim. 3:16–17, GW)
- "In every way I showed you [_____] that by working hard like this we can help those who are weak. We must remember what the Lord Jesus said, 'We are more happy when we give than when we receive.'" (Acts 20:35, NLV)

- I [_____] work hard and struggle for this goal with his energy, which works in me powerfully. (Col. 1:29, CEB)
- No matter how much you want, laziness won't help a bit, but hard work will reward you [_____] with more than enough. (Prov. 13:4, CEV)
- Whatever presents itself for you [_____] to do, do it with all your might. (Eccl. 9:10, GW)
- "Get up [_____]! It's your duty to take action. We are with you, so be strong and take action." (Ezra 10:4, GW)
- And let us not get tired of doing what is right, for after a while we [_____] will reap a harvest of blessing if we don't get discouraged and give up. (Gal. 6:9, TLB)
- [_____] Keep your eyes on Jesus, our leader and instructor. (Heb. 12:2, TLB)
- May this God of peace prepare you [_____] to do every good thing he wants. May he work in us through Jesus Christ to do what is pleasing to him. Glory belongs to Jesus Christ forever. Amen. (Heb. 13:21, GW)
- [_____] The person with understanding is always looking for wisdom, but the mind of a fool wanders everywhere. (Prov. 17:24, NCV)
- Humble yourselves [_____] in the Lord's presence. Then he will give you a high position. (James 4:10, GW)
- Be glad you [_____] can do the things you should be doing. Do all things without arguing and talking about how you wish you did not have to do them. (Phil. 2:14, NLV)
- I [_____] am happy to do your will, O my God. Your teachings are deep within me. (Ps. 40:8, GW)
- In those days when you [_____] pray, I will listen. You will find me when you seek me, if you look for me in earnest. (Jer. 29:12–13, TLB)
- [_____] Hard work means prosperity; only a fool idles away his time. (Prov. 12:11, TLB)

PART 5

LEADERSHIP ATTRIBUTE: RENEWING

Create in me a clean heart, O God, and renew a right spirit within me.

PSALM 51:10 ESV

ATTRIBUTE AFFIRMATION:
I CREATE SPACE FOR GOD TO WORK IN MY BODY, MIND,
AND SPIRIT TO CONTINUALLY LIVE IN HEALTH
AND WHOLENESS.

CHAPTER SIXTEEN

FIRE POKER PROTECTION: SUSTAINABLE SPIRITUAL FORMATION

We have to keep looking for the spiritual question if we want spiritual answers.

—HENRI NOUWEN

"Which window is broken?" my dad asked as my aunt led him from the garage into the laundry room. I watched as she turned and held up our four-foot brass fire poker as she answered him calmly but firmly, "It's the window above the washer and dryer. When I arrived on Friday to take care of the house, I noticed the window pane was crooked. When I tried to get it closed, I realized the lock was broken. Because it kept bothering me, I've slept every night down here on the couch by that window holding this fire poker. I feel uneasy, and it needs to get repaired."

My dad was mildly amused. He formed a half smile, drew in a long breath, and then politely answered her. "Well Marie, you've survived African jungles and witch doctors. You've overcome polio and traveled the world, so if you tell me you're uneasy and are sleeping with that fire poker to protect yourself, I just have to say I'm impressed!" She looked a little perturbed. Aunt Marie was a strong single woman, used to taking care of herself, and everyone else, too.

Dad sensed her exasperation so he quickly continued, "I meant to say I'll make a point to get the window lock repaired tomorrow. Thanks for showing me the broken lock. And, thanks for staying here at the house while we were gone." Marie's body language said to me she felt relieved.

Somehow it seemed she had completed her mission regarding that window. Then she marched up the stairs to the kitchen, put the poker back onto the hearth, and picked up her coat to head back to her apartment.

It was already late. For a fifteen-year-old teenager, I thought it had been an agonizingly long ride home from Yakima to Tacoma across the icy mountain pass. For hours all six of us had been crammed into our little car, including my parents, two sisters, and one little brother who always managed to get into the front seat. We were returning from Thanksgiving holidays, which included attending our statewide youth convention. Hundreds of teenagers from across the Pacific Northwest had attended with us. My thirteen-year-old sister, Kathie, and I had loved every minute of the contemporary worship and preaching, but now we were exhausted.

For the whole family, it was lights out by 10:30 p.m. As I climbed into my bed, I looked across at Kathie, who was already asleep in her parallel twin bed. As I nodded off, in my head I replayed Dad's conversation with Aunt Marie. It was all so odd to me.

Suddenly I was awake. The moonlight cascading through the window gave enough light to see clearly, but I couldn't believe what I saw! Standing at the foot of my bed was the silhouette of a tall, Caucasian, dark-haired man. In the first split second, I must have moved. I don't really know. But in the next second, he disappeared. I thought to myself *I must be mistaken.* It had to be my imagination. However, in the next second, as I looked across to my sleeping sister, I realized the man was on his hands and knees crawling in between our beds—toward me.

"Dad! Dad! Dad!" I shrieked in horror, at full volume. The man on the floor instantly jumped up and ran into the hallway. He catapulted down the stairs to the kitchen, then down the stairs to the family room, and finally out the back door down the hill. My father, who was sleeping with Mom in the next bedroom, was up like a shot chasing the intruder with a baseball bat! Continuing to scream, I followed them both down the staircases. But now the entire family was out of their rooms yelling.

My poor father, baseball bat in hand and in his underwear, came back inside from his efforts to find the intruder. I was hysterical. As my parents tried to calm me down, Mom discovered where the intruder had come into the house.

Yes. He had crawled in through the laundry room window over the washer and dryer. It was still standing open. On that window sill, many small rocks had been carefully laid out to spell "I love you." It was a chilling message to me. I was terrified and in shock.

Then I remembered that unusual exchange between my father and Auntie Marie earlier that evening. Suddenly, it was strangely reassuring and calming. The Holy Spirit had warned my aunt. Dad had gone to bed with a baseball bat. God was taking care of me.

Yes, it was very traumatic. No one ever confessed. We called the police, but the case was never solved. Dad eventually concluded for himself on the identity of the intruder. However, something more important and eternal had changed in me forever. I had witnessed the spiritual leading of the Holy Spirit in my aunt's life. I had discovered it was possible to hear the voice of God—if I would just listen.

God wants to talk to each of us. He created us to be in a listening relationship with Him. As we take the time to practice solitude, silence, and prayer, we will hear God's voice. We will receive affirmation, encouragement, correction, and direction for our lives from the Holy Spirit. Jesus told a story to explain how this works. He said,

> The thief comes only to steal and kill and destroy. I came that they may have life and have it abundantly. I am the good shepherd. The good shepherd lays down his life for the sheep. He who is a hired hand and not a shepherd, who does not own the sheep, sees the wolf coming and leaves the sheep and flees, and the wolf snatches them and scatters them. He flees because he is a hired hand and cares nothing for the sheep. I am the good shepherd. I know my own and my own know me, just as the Father knows me and I know the Father; and I lay down my life for the sheep (John 10:10–15, ESV).

Jesus said that we are His sheep and He is our Shepherd. He cares for us

> As we take
> the time
> to practice
> solitude,
> silence,
> and prayer,
> we will
> hear God's
> voice.

and protects us just like an ancient Israeli shepherd would defend his flock from predators. Because the people listening to Jesus were familiar with tending sheep, Jesus knew the disciples would understand His meaning. Every good Jewish shepherd cultivated a personal relationship with his flock so they would follow him just by listening to his voice. Jesus emphasized that His sheep would also listen to His voice (John 10:16).

We want to listen with our whole hearts to receive His supernatural guidance. When we turn our attention upward, our focus changes from earthly distractions. Then God's voice can become loud enough for us to hear.

SPIRITUAL FORMATION THROUGH SPIRITUAL DISCIPLINES

As you become a Spirit-empowered leader, you can take several actions to cooperate with God's leading. These are called disciplines of spiritual formation. The progression of spiritual formation is outlined in various passages of the New Testament. It's most fully spelled out in 2 Peter 1:4–7,

> Through these he has given us his very great and precious promises, so that through them you may participate in the divine nature, having escaped the corruption in the world caused by evil desires. For this very reason, make every effort to add to your faith goodness; and to goodness, knowledge; and to knowledge, self-control; and to self-control, perseverance; and to perseverance, godliness; and to godliness, mutual affection, and to mutual affection, love.

The world *needs* each one of us to be fully alive and growing in love, character, and the lifestyle of Jesus! To do that, we need the power of the Holy Spirit. Connecting to that power requires practicing spiritual disciplines that allow the Holy Spirit to work through us and to empower us.

By themselves, these actions are nothing but busy work. When we approach them as spiritual disciplines and utilize them as part of our spiritual walk, they become a direct action to help us connect with the blessings and will of God.

> When you open your heart, you invite God in to do *amazing* things in your life!

God's power is made perfect in our weakness (2 Cor. 12:9) and becomes visible through our growth. This means our path to leadership must always be directed by a humble dependence on God. Let me say it this way: Your *heart* needs to be fully involved in this process of spiritual growth. Open your heart during the times of prayer and solitude. Approach your spiritual growth plan and Bible study with an open heart. When you open your heart, you invite God in to do *amazing* things in your life!

DISCIPLINES OF THE HOLY SPIRIT

The disciplines of the Holy Spirit help us draw near to God, reach out for Him, and give up our earthly encumbrances. They help us become more like Jesus while growing into the heart of God.

Blessings of Being Filled with the Holy Spirit
- Greater love and intimacy with God
- Exaltation of Jesus as the Son of God and Savior
- Power and boldness to witness and preach
- Greater wisdom and faith
- Deep joy

For Your Spirit—Disciplines of Surrender
The disciplines of surrender strengthen God's authority in our lives.
- Repentance and confession
- Yielding and submission
- Worship

For Your Mind—Disciplines of Solitude
The disciplines of solitude help us grow closer to God by choosing to be intentionally alone with Him, away from human interaction and distraction.

- Solitude and silence
- Listening and guidance
- Prayer and intercession
- Study and meditation

For Your Body—Disciplines of Service and Sanctification
Your body is the temple of the Holy Spirit and is a gift to be stewarded. The act of fellowship, connecting with other believers, also connects us to the Holy Spirit. The relationships we intentionally build directly impact our relationship with God.

- Fellowship
- Simplicity
- Service
- Witness
- Fasting
- Health

Nothing could be a more important leadership attribute than hearing God's direction and wisdom in our everyday lives. The Spirit-filled life is the Christ-directed life, by which Jesus lives His life through us in the power of the Holy Spirit. Jesus promised we would have powerful, loving, abundant, and fruitful lives as a result of being filled with the Holy Spirit. The world needs women leaders in ministry who are growing into the love, character, and lifestyle of Jesus Christ.

To be an effective leader, your testimony to the power of God's living presence in your life is the greatest attribute you'll ever need. Demonstrations of hearing God's leading in times of testing will galvanize your influence in any situation. God primarily speaks through His Word. "Every part of Scripture is God-breathed and useful one way or another—showing us truth, exposing our rebellion, correcting our mistakes, training us to live God's way. Through the Word we are put together and shaped up for the tasks God has for us" (2 Tim. 3:16–17, MSG). Being led by the Spirit will bring you greater intimacy with God, power, boldness to speak your faith, quiet confidence during opposition, a deeper trust in Scripture as the Word of God, and a fresh love for Christ and others.

MOVING FROM SURVIVING TO THRIVING

In Matthew 16:26, Jesus said it is possible to gain everything we want in our lives but lose our soul. As a woman leader, it is possible to gain the world of ministry success and lose your soul in the midst of it all. When women leaders lose their souls, so do their families and the organizations and churches where they serve. Strengthening your soul of leadership is an invitation to enter more deeply into the process of spiritual formation, and then to purposefully lead from that place. It's a chance to construct a connection between your soul and your leadership rather than experiencing them as separate domains of your life.

Spiritual formation is impossible for you to accomplish on your own. It can only be done through God's supernatural guidance and intervention. However, knowing that you don't have to change yourself is a huge relief. By simply moving forward in the journey of your ministry calling with an open heart to hearing God's voice through your obstacles, God will meet you at your point of need.

Your only responsibility is to make yourself available to encounter His presence each day. The choice to lead from our place of need is a vulnerable, transparent position. It's a place where we don't have all the answers and have given control to God. As Scott Peck said, "The truth is that our finest moments are most likely to occur when we are feeling deeply uncomfortable, unhappy, or unfulfilled. For it is only in such moments, propelled by our discomfort, that we are likely to step out of our ruts and start searching for different ways or truer answers."

God dwells at your point of need. By staying focused on Him, you are freed from the expectations of others and your personal compulsions to be enamored with human voices. You are freed from the addiction

> To be an effective leader, your testimony to the power of God's living presence in your life is the greatest attribute you'll ever need.

of accomplishment and pushing for perfection or status. Believing that God loves you creates an inner freedom to slacken your grip on things—money, success, relationships—that have defined you. When we have faced ourselves and discovered God's love is greater than any of our shortcomings, we can lead with liberty and abandonment because we have nothing to lose. This place of security will give you something real to offer those who seek your leadership.

The more spiritual the destination, the greater the importance of integrity. Behaviors and attitudes from previous years may have been good enough in the past, but not for the next stretch of your road. There is a price to be paid for leadership. God's power is made perfect in our weakness (2. Cor. 12:9) and becomes visible through our growth. This means our path to leadership must always be directed by a humble dependence on God.

TRANSFORMATION

Transformation is indispensable. Life is composed of continued transformations, as individuals move from one stage to another. Actually, transformation is one of the major components that make up life. "If we aren't constantly being transformed, changed to the better, we actually lose our life."[1] Transformation captures both the process and the product of Christian discipleship.[2] Spiritual transformation is a process in which we move from the person we are to a person who is being transformed into the image of Christ (2 Cor. 3:16–18).

THINGS TO CONSIDER:

1. Describe an event in your life where you could clearly see the Holy Spirit at work.

    _____

    _____

    _____

2. How do you actively practice spiritual formation in your life?

    _____

    _____

    _____

3. What spiritual disciplines do you feel you should focus on to strengthen you as you pursue your leadership goals?

    _____

    _____

    _____

4. Do you feel you are surviving or thriving in your life and ministry?

    _____

5. Are you willing to begin a process of spiritual transformation, growing closer to God and allowing the Holy Spirit to work freely in your life? How will doing this change your leadership?

    _____

    _____

    _____

    _____

CHAPTER SEVENTEEN

WOMEN WHO THINK TOO MUCH

Finally, brothers and sisters, whatever is true, whatever is noble, whatever is right, whatever is pure, whatever is lovely, whatever is admirable—if anything is excellent or praiseworthy—think about such things.

—PHILIPPIANS 4:8

Attitude can't be hidden. It's the state of your spirit and mind that influences your choices, which determines your words and your actions. Attitude is tangible. We can't control our life circumstances, but we can choose to control our attitudes and reactions to our situations. God has given us the ability to stand outside of ourselves and evaluate our thoughts. You can stand on God's Word to capture toxic thoughts by counteracting them with godly wisdom.

The truth is you can't change yesterday. It's over, along with its mistakes, disappointments, and failures. That includes both your mistakes and the failures of others. You can't have a *do over*. It's gone. But, if you allow the pain of yesterday to spill into your today, you poison your potential for positive forward results in your leadership, and in your life. Jesus taught us to forgive not seven times, but seventy-seven times (Matt. 18:21–23). He was overstating to His audience, emphasizing the point that we are to forgive endlessly.

Research in recent years has proven that your mental, emotional, and physical health will increase when you forgive every day.[1] You will live longer and enjoy life more if you start activating greater forgiveness for

SHATTERING THE STAINED GLASS CEILING

yourself, for your circumstances, and for others.

Forgiveness is *releasing*. Jesus taught what modern science is only now confirming: Forgiveness only occurs when you let go of your negative emotions, thoughts, or behaviors about a situation or person who has wronged you. In place of the negative emotions, you respond with kindness, generosity, and compassion.[2]

Unforgiveness is hanging on to pain. Each time you bring the hurt back into consciousness it changes, getting either worse or better—this is up to you. It's difficult to let go of unjust things that have happened to you, but those thoughts get worse with more of your attention. The common, worldly approach is to indulge, speak about, tear apart, and wallow in the unfair treatment you have received. However, this doesn't bring healing. You have the power to acknowledge unforgiveness and repent. Then you must consciously release the situation/person into God's hands. You can't control the event, but you can control your reaction to the event. Repentance and forgiveness stop worry and anxiety and acknowledge God's sovereignty, putting Him back on the throne to do what He will do.

WORRY, ANXIETY, AND FORGIVENESS

"Robyn, I'm sorry to say but your husband has three to seven years to live." I almost dropped my phone. "What? This can't be true!" I shouted loudly over the boat engines. My seemingly healthy husband, Rich, had been undergoing tests and now a hematologist was stating Rich's prognosis in an irritated, exasperated tone.

"Look, it's terrible news. I have to go." Terror shot through my mind. My thoughts screamed, *Doctor, what do you mean you have to go? I need to know lots more information. Can't you stay on the phone and talk to me? How insensitive and cruel can you be?* However, he hung up anyway.

It was Friday evening, long after business hours, on a hot July evening. My husband and our four sons were out in our boat enjoying the sun and warm ocean. I had put in a message to ask the physician to call me when he had the results of Rich's blood work, but the doctor was irritated that I had requested a call back so late on a Friday. When my cell phone rang, I didn't anticipate this kind of conversation or this diagnosis. Our youngest son was only nine years old, and the other three teen boys certainly needed their dad. We had just taken on our Miami mission. I cannot exaggerate how distraught I was at that moment.

I was anxious and couldn't sleep. Worry began to overwhelm me. I had chest pains. However, when I told my mother-in-law about the doctor's prognosis, she said to me, "Robyn, we will pray. God has it under control. One day at a time."

I was stunned. I wondered how she could be so calm. I had a lot to learn. As time evolved, we researched more about Rich's blood disorder and discovered that although it was a chronic condition, it was manageable. When Rich went for a second opinion, the new hematologist said, "Well, I can't imagine any doctor telling Robyn what he did. He painted the prognosis in the worst possible scenario. This disease is certainly serious, but together we can work to keep Rich healthy for many years to come!"

The toxic conversation with Rich's doctor took place sixteen years ago, and my husband is active, strong, and living life to the fullest. Lesson? If you don't like the prognosis, get another doctor. Deeper lesson? Don't waste worry on things that only God can handle. Since that time, I've created mental fences in my mind, boundaries for active thinking. Worry, anxiety, and fear are only allowed to fly around for a few flutters but never to land. Gratitude for today and belief that God will work everything out in my favor is the formula. In addition, most of the things I've ever worried about never happened. Worry only limits our joy and distracts us from God's solutions.

WOMEN WHO THINK TOO MUCH

A young mother was walking along the seashore with her young son. Suddenly a huge wave came crashing to shore and sucked the little boy out to sea. The mother became hysterical and dropped to her knees, threw her hands in the air and cried out to God, "Help me! Please send my boy

> Worry only limits our joy and distracts us from God's solutions.

back. I will do anything if you just send my boy back." And with the rhythm of the next wave, her son was washed back up on shore. There he stood next to her safe and sound, but dripping wet. With that, the young mom looked back up to heaven and said, "Well, he had a hat!"

Are you smiling? Do you recognize yourself in this fictitious story? Many of us are never happy, no matter how many prayers God answers for us. We work, we pray, we get results, but somehow things are never quite right. We are never fully content with ourselves or the people around us. We get caught in a torrent of negative thoughts and emotions that interfere with our well being. A coworker makes a casual remark about your new shoes, and you spend the next half hour wondering if she really liked them or if she was sarcastic.

Most women readily identify with this kind of internal self-talk: *What's wrong with me? Why am I never satisfied with what I'm doing? Nothing ever feels quite right. Maybe it's my hormones. But it seems like I feel this way all month long. Maybe I made the wrong decision. I tell people I like my work, but I feel so conflicted.*

This kind of obsessive thinking seems to plague women more than men. Some of the most gifted, educated, well-dressed women leaders I've ever met are also the most unhappy and the most frustrated. In spite of their success, they don't seem to enjoy life and the fruit of all their hard work. From early adolescence through adulthood, women are twice as likely as men to experience depression.[3] When we strain to overcome this trap, it's like trying to escape from emotional quicksand.

No doubt your stress is real, and your problems seem to never end. We all deal with challenges and difficulties, often on a daily basis. It's exhausting to navigate the stormy waters of life, but I want to encourage you right now—you aren't in your boat alone!

Nothing is more overwhelming than believing that all the challenges of life are your responsibility. God loves you and is fully aware of every circumstance you are facing right now. Your choice is to trust yourself or to trust Him. When you trust God, this doesn't release you from responsibilities or obligations; it simply means you aren't facing those decisions alone. Today you can stop carrying your load all by yourself. Go to the Lord and ask Him to take control. You may need to be patient, but He is always faithful.

GOD WANTS TO GIVE YOU A RICH LIFE

Life is lived in the "dash" between your birth date and your death date. The average life span is now 27,375 days. It sounds like a lot, but you can do your own calculation. I do know this: every day matters.

Decades ago I quit college to get married. I didn't understand that quitting would mean I would have so many responsibilities in the coming years that I wouldn't be able to get back to my education. Kids, husband, and ministry took up all of my time and energy. But just because you fail at reaching your goal right away doesn't mean you won't get there eventually. I quit college back then, and now I have finished a doctorate!

I find it fascinating that the cells of our bodies are renewed every seven years. That means every cell in your body is remade. You are not even the same person you were ten years ago—not physically and not spiritually. The key is to keep on going, to keep moving forward. Never lose sight of your vision and goals.

You can stay out of the trap of worry and panic by believing God has a better life in store for you: a life full of laughter, contentment, provision, peace, and joy. Anytime we don't put God first, life gets messy and we become stressed out. Our part is to trust God; His part is to provide the answer we need!

Having a deep confidence that God is working in your life will keep you from panicking when you face the next crisis. With God on your side, you can't lose. If you decide not to push the panic button, God will give you the calm confidence to walk through any storm with peace and poise. Whatever you may face, God has already taken care of it.

> If you decide not to push the panic button, God will give you the calm confidence to walk through any storm with peace and poise.

RENEWING

Today, women are carrying enormous loads at home and in the workplace. In your leadership skills toolbox, you already have the active leadership attributes of mission, reframing, connecting, and engaging, but without *renewing* your energy you will be too limited to accomplish anything. Leadership takes a toll on every woman in every profession. Women now make up half of the workforce in the United States, but working moms still take on the bulk of household chores.[4] Studies reveal a growing modern workplace trend "engendering a long hours culture where 'being present' is valued as a sign of commitment to work."[5]

Stressed, tired, and rushed have become the description of the modern family in America.[6] When women add their extra load of family and household responsibilities[7] to their professional work-week, it's easy to understand why so many experience burnout.[8] Although women today have tremendous new opportunities, some of the same old challenges remain. Women are totally exhausted, have too much to do, and have too little time.

You are body, mind, and spirit. Being on mission, implementing your strategies, reframing the obstacles along the way, connecting inspirationally with your family and team, and engaging in your work will all come to a grinding halt unless you discover your key to sustainable renewable energy. No wonder you fall into bed totally spent night after night. The cycle is relentless, and you can yearn for a break in the action. So when you meet other working women, the questions on your mind are *How do they get it all done? What is my missing ingredient?*

Start by rethinking the concept of balance between your personal/home schedules and your professional ministry work. Most women tend to assume that being out of balance is the cause of energy issues because conventional wisdom says home time is restorative and work time is draining. In reality things aren't so black and white.

The wrong kind of home time can be crippling. Think of endless diapers, screaming teenagers, empty refrigerators, piles of laundry, or a needy husband. You experience a teeter-totter of energy ups and downs in every part of your life whether at home or work. Also, there are intense seasons of being at home with small children or ailing family members. You might also face work-related key events or projects that require an avalanche of overtime. Balance is tough to define.

As busy women leaders we share a hugely seductive notion that some woman, somewhere, has the secret formula to handling everything in her world efficiently and effortlessly. You look around and think you've failed to crack the code. Relax—there is no code! There is no perfect balance in human planning. But women leaders we know do take vacations, have a happy family, and are glowing with health—so how do they do it?

First, let go of the mind-set that you can reach a constant state of total control. Only God can initiate perfect balance. Give Him your schedule and commit your home time and your work time to Him. He can expand and balance what you will never be able to stabilize.

Next, replace your vision with a new plan of managing your own *energy flow* inside the framework of what is important to you—at the time. By reframing the challenge this way, you are replacing an unsolvable problem (sustaining a work/life equilibrium state) with a big payoff: never running your energy batteries on empty. That's when you're most vulnerable, most likely to make mistakes, and you lose the joy of leadership. Energy plays a huge role in your success.

LIMITING BELIEFS CAN HOLD YOU BACK

A newly married bride started to prepare dinner when her groom walked into the kitchen. She reached for the large beef roast, and then to the astonishment of her husband she cut off both ends and threw them in the garbage. He was incredulous. "Why are you doing that?" he shouted. She

SHATTERING THE STAINED GLASS CEILING

smiled warmly and confidently replied, "Well, my mom makes the best pot roast in our city, and that's what she always does."

So the groom shrugged and walked away. Years later his mother-in-law was in the same kitchen, and she was preparing dinner. As she picked up the beef roast, she placed it into the pot and began to add seasonings. The young husband said, "Aren't you going to cut off the ends of the roast? Your daughter does it every time, and she says that is your secret recipe." The mother-in-law dropped her jaw and gasped, "Oh no! The reason I cut the ends off all those years was that I never owned a pot big enough to fit the roast!"

That young bride was only imitating a solution to her mother's problem! How many unconscious assumptions are you making in your life? These constraints can be described as limiting beliefs that hold us back. They are conscious or unconscious beliefs or assumptions that limit what you do and how you think. When we operate within our relationships with people, we often make an assumption that they hold the same viewpoints, opinions, or beliefs we have. Most assumed constraints are below the surface. It's important to surface them in yourself and the people you lead.

REST: LETTING GO TO REST IN GOD'S BIG PLAN FOR YOU

Exhausted? What problems and obstacles are you trying to solve in your life? How are you going about it? Working out the solution with worry is not the way to get your best answer. Research indicates that our conscious thought is better at making linear analytic decisions, but unconscious thought is especially effective at solving complex problems. Unconscious thinking—when you are focused on something other than the problem—may provide inspirational sparks that eventually lead to important discoveries.[9] So the key to unlocking our unconscious processes is taking the time to *not think* about the challenge. In other words, engage all of your mental resources and achieve those moments of inspiration you need to shut your brain off!

Think about the biggest challenge you face, the one that has been plaguing you. How do you come up with the answer to your impossible situation? Instead of beating your head against a wall, or spending countless hours trying to solve this issue, just stop. Take a break from your daily stream of family and ministry. Let go. Turn your attention and thoughts upward through prayer and meditation.

A good night's sleep equips us to be more effective in our leadership. Without renewing our minds and our bodies with adequate rest, we rob ourselves of effectiveness. God has promised rest without tossing and turning. "When you lie down, you will not be afraid; when you lie down, your sleep will be sweet" (Prov. 3:24, AMP). Your sleep is your reward for working hard. It's essential to give your body, mind, and spirit time to renew.

In the first chapter of Genesis, God sets the boundary by telling us He rested on the seventh day of creation. Taking a day off is honoring the Sabbath God put in place. To live a healthy life, we need to value rest. A real day off means turning your attention away from your worries, setting a boundary on all problems, and letting go with your conscious mind. Your day off is meant to revitalize you so you can return to your work with passion. Jesus intended for us to work hard and then to rest when He said, "Come to Me, all who are weary and heavily burdened . . . and I will give you rest" (Matt. 11:28, AMP). Never be so busy you forget to just stop.

THINGS TO CONSIDER:

1. Identify one toxic thought in your life. How is it affecting your life? How can you remove that thought from your life?

    _____

    _____

    _____

    _____

2. Is unforgiveness holding you back in any relationship? What do you need to do to remove that block from your life?

    _____

    _____

    _____

    _____

3. Think about your self talk. Is it positive and affirming or negative and undermining? Write out three affirming statements you can make to yourself every day.

    • _____

    • _____

    • _____

4. Write down an issue you are facing that you feel is out of your control.

    _____

    _____

5. Now take a moment and pray about that issue, releasing it to God, and realize that *He has this*!

CHAPTER EIGHTEEN

COACHING: DEVELOPING BOUNDLESS ENERGY

May God himself, the God who makes everything holy and whole, make
you holy and whole, put you together—spirit, soul, and body—and keep
you fit for the coming of our Master, Jesus Christ.

—1 THESSALONIANS 5:23-24, MSG

Boundless energy is available to you as you allow your body, mind, and spirit to
be transformed. Spiritual formation is less about dispensing information and
more about asking questions. Jesus asked 307 questions in Scripture. You must
let go of bitterness and forgiveness and open yourself to growth.

COACHING QUESTIONS: BOUNDLESS ENERGY

1.   Where do you see God most at work in your life?
2.   Where are you growing the most?
3.   What fruit of the Spirit is most abundant in your life?
4.   What fruit of the Spirit is least abundant in your life?
5.   What changes do you want to make in your life that only God
     can make?
6.   What is God teaching you right now?
7.   What is stopping you from doing what you know God has called
     you to do?
8.   What do you want?
9.   Where is God in that situation?

10. How does the Bible address that?
11. What do you see in the Scriptures that leads you to that conclusion?
12. What about ministry gets you really excited?
13. How are you and God doing?
14. How is God developing your character?

COACHING EXERCISE: INVENTORY FOR YOUR ENERGY

Check the statements below that are true.

Body

_____ Regularly, I don't get enough sleep, and I often wake up feeling tired.

_____ I usually skip breakfast, or just grab something that isn't nutritious.

_____ I don't work out enough (meaning cardiovascular training at least three times a week and strength training at least once a week).

_____ I don't take regular breaks during the day to renew and recharge, or I often eat lunch at my desk, if I eat it at all.

Mind

_____ I have difficulty focusing and I'm easily distracted by digital communication and e-mail.

_____ I spend too much of my day reacting to the immediate crisis rather than focusing on activities with longer-term value and high leverage.

_____ I don't take enough time for creative reflection and development.

_____ I almost never take an e-mail–free vacation.

_____ Emotionally, I'm upset often.

_____ I don't have enough time with my family and loved ones, and when I'm with them, I'm not really "present."

_____ I have too little time for the activities I enjoy most.

_____ I don't stop often enough to express my appreciation to others or to savor my accomplishments and blessings.

Spirit

_____ In my ministry work I don't spend enough time working in my strengths.

_____ I don't regularly participate in a weekly worship service.

_____ I don't have a daily time of prayer and meditation.

_____ There are substantial cracks between what I say is most important to me in my life and how I distribute my energy and time.

_____ My ministry doesn't reflect my calling.

_____ My decisions at work are more often induced by outside demands than by a clear sense of my purpose.

_____ I don't invest enough time and energy in making a positive difference to others or the world.

How is your overall energy? Total number of statements checked:

_____

Guide to Scores

0–3: Excellent energy management skills

4–6: Reasonable energy management skills

7–10: Significant energy management deficits

11–16: A full-fledged energy management crisis

What Do You Need to Work On?

Number of checks in each category:

Body _____

Mind _____

Spirit _____

Guide to Score
0: Excellent energy management skills
1: Strong energy management skills
2: Significant deficits
3: Poor energy management skills
4: A full-fledged energy crisis

COACHING EXERCISE: PERSONAL RETREAT

Set aside time to take an individual spiritual retreat for at least one day. The purpose of the retreat is prayer, Scripture study and meditation, journaling, and reflecting on your life and ministry. This is a time to disconnect from the outside world and allow God to speak to you about your leadership and your life. Keep a journal of reflections during your retreat.

COACHING QUESTIONS: RENEWAL

Body
1. How do your beliefs, attitudes, and practices have a positive impact on your health?
2. Where do you rate health in your life? Low, medium, or high priority?
3. While keeping your *life mission* in focus, how do your exercise and eating habits work into your strategy?
4. Rate your nutrition on a scale of 1–10 (1=very poor, 10=excellent).
5. List three areas of your nutrition that would like to improve.
6. In order to be satisfied with your eating/exercise, what would need to change in your life?
7. What are your eating habits?
8. When you decide what to eat, what do you consider?
9. How many glasses of water do you consume daily?

10. How deliberate are you about your grooming and hygiene?

11. On a scale of 1–10, how would you rate your present fitness level (1=worst, 10=best)?

12. What is your routine for fitness? Physical exercise?

13. How much rest are you getting? Do you get enough sleep? If not, why?

14. To make the necessary lifestyle changes to reach your health goals, rate how committed you are on a scale of 1–10, with 10 as the "most committed."

15. When will you set up your annual physical with your physician?

Mind

1. What steps can you take to create a daily time for quiet meditation and prayer?

2. To overcome anxiety and stress, what actions can you take?

3. For your most restful sleep, what steps can you implement to improve your bedtime routine?

4. What do you say about yourself?

5. Do you take breaks during your day?

6. What brings stress into your life?

7. How do you manage your stress?

8. What refreshes you, mentally?

9. To get more peace, what one change could you make to your lifestyle?

10. What's one way you could have more fun in your life?

11. What are your hobbies?

12. What's a new hobby that would interest you?

13. Who around you makes you laugh?

14. To have more peace in your finances, what's one thing that you could do?

15. How do your thought patterns impact your emotions, feelings, and associated behaviors?

Spirit

1. On a scale of 1–10, how is your prayer life? (1=very poor, 10=excellent)
2. How often do you spend time reading the Bible?
3. After reading the Bible, how do you apply it to your life?
4. How often do you spend time in silent solitude (refraining from interacting with other people) to be alone with God?
5. How do feel about fasting? Explain why.
6. When was the last time you fasted?
7. When do you spend time worshipping God and praising His greatness and goodness with words, music, and song?
8. How consistently do you attend a church service? (Ministry can take us out of participating.)
9. How often do you invite others to church?
10. How important is it for you to share your faith with others?
11. How do you share your faith with others?
12. When do you share your faith with others?
13. What steps can you take to increase how often you share your faith with others?
14. How do you feel after you share your faith with others?
15. How do people respond when you share your faith with them?

POSITIVE POWER PRAYER:
COACHING FROM THE INSIDE OUT

God's *renewing* for you is already at work, but to increase your awareness of the Holy Spirit in your life, it's important that you base your intention on God's Word. *Focused attention* is like a muscle that you can strengthen through exercise. Begin with a prayer of thanksgiving. *Be grateful* for where you are in your life today. Read one Scripture out loud and insert your first name into the sentence. As you speak the Scripture, declare the promise and reframe your circumstances into a positive outcome with a hopeful future. Stop. Now, do it again. Your *renewing* is creating space for God to work in you. As you think through your personal process of connecting, focus on these Scriptures and speak to your future:

- I praise you because I [_____] am fearfully and wonderfully made; your works are wonderful, I know that full well. (Ps. 139:14)
- She [_____] puts on strength like a belt and goes to work with energy. (Prov. 31:17, GW)
- Do you not know that your body [_____] is a house of God where the Holy Spirit lives? God gave you His Holy Spirit. Now you belong to God. You do not belong to yourselves. God bought you with a great price. So [_____] honor God with your body. You belong to Him. (1 Cor. 6:19–20, NLV)
- He fills my [_____] life with good things. My youth is renewed like the eagle's! (Ps. 103:5, NLT)
- The LORD your God is with you [_____]. He is a hero who saves you. He happily rejoices over you [_____], renews you with his love, and celebrates over you with shouts of joy. (Zeph. 3:17, GW)
- "My grace is sufficient for you [_____] [My loving kindness and My mercy are more than enough—always available—regardless of the situation]; for [My] power is being perfected [and is completed and shows itself most effectively] in [your] weakness." Therefore, I will all the more gladly boast in my weaknesses, so that the power of Christ [may completely enfold me and] may dwell in me. (2 Cor. 12:9, AMP)
- GOD makes his people strong [_____]. God gives his people peace. (Ps. 29:11, MSG)
- All of us, then, reflect the glory of the Lord with uncovered faces; and that same glory, coming from the Lord, who is the Spirit, transforms us [_____] into his likeness in an ever greater degree of glory. (2 Cor. 3:18, GNT)
- [_____] Kind words are like honey—sweet to the taste and good for your health. (Prov. 16:24, GNT)
- We [_____] are his servants because the same God who said that light should shine out of darkness has given us light. For that reason we bring to light the knowledge about God's glory which

shines from Christ's face. (2 Cor. 4:6, GW)

- [_____] A tranquil heart makes for a healthy body, but jealousy is like bone cancer. (Prov. 14:30, GW)

- Planted in the house of the LORD, they [I, _____] will flourish in the courts of our God. (Ps. 92:13, AMP)

- That is why we [_____] are not discouraged. Though outwardly we are wearing out, inwardly we are renewed day by day. (2 Cor. 4:16, GW)

- He refreshes and restores my [_____'s] soul (life); He leads me in the paths of righteousness for His name's sake. (Ps. 23:3, AMP)

- Therefore, I urge you, brothers and sisters [_____], in view of God's mercy, to offer your bodies as a living sacrifice, holy and pleasing to God—this is your true and proper worship. Do not conform to the pattern of this world, but be transformed by the renewing of your mind. (Rom. 12:1–2)

- [_____] This means that anyone who belongs to Christ has become a new person. The old life is gone; a new life has begun! (2 Cor. 5:17, NLT)

- Don't worry about anything [_____], but pray about everything. With thankful hearts offer up your prayers and requests to God. Then, because you [_____] belong to Christ Jesus, God will bless you with peace that no one can completely understand. And this peace will control the way you think and feel. (Phil. 4:6–7, CEV)

- [_____] My friends, God has made us these promises. So we should stay away from everything that keeps our bodies and spirits from being clean. We should honor God and try to be completely like him. (2 Cor. 7:1, CEV)

- Be careful how you think; your life [_____] is shaped by your thoughts. (Prov. 4:23, GNT)

- We [_____] break down every thought and proud thing that puts itself up against the wisdom of God. We take hold of every thought and make it obey Christ. (2 Cor. 10:5, NLV)

- [_____] Don't be lazy in showing your devotion. Use your energy to serve the Lord. (Rom. 12:11, GW)

- God is faithful and reliable. If we [_____] confess our sins, he forgives them and cleanses us from everything we've done wrong. (1 John 1:9, GW)
- Now your attitudes and thoughts [_____] must all be constantly changing for the better. Yes, you must be a new and different person, holy and good. Clothe yourself with this new nature. (Eph. 4:23–24, TLB)

CONCLUSION

"I have told you these things, so that in me you may have peace.
In this world you will have trouble. But take heart! I have overcome the
world."

—JOHN 16:33

We cannot predict the future, but we can create it.[1] Think back and consider what has happened for women in your world, in your country, in the markets, in your work, and in your life that defied all expectations. God wants to defy expectations in your life, too. He called you to be a leader, and now it's time to move in that direction. Seize the day, because this is your day!

BE FULLY ALIVE

Owning your life mission, setting a forward direction in your thinking, identifying goals, and then engaging in your quest is the certain pathway to your long-term success. Your essential leadership attributes are the keys to growing your capacity. Now is the time to make every day count. Stop living your life as if your goal is only to arrive safely at death. We all know tomorrow is not guaranteed, so make today count.

"I am a leader.

I am a person of influence.

Today I choose to be a blessing.

With God's help there is nothing I cannot accomplish.

Instead of being reactive, I will be proactive.

I know the answer.

I am the solution."[2]

This statement of leadership is your first breakthrough to shattering your stained glass ceiling.

KEEP ASKING

Through this leadership coaching strategy, I pray that you have begun to value your own success. You will escalate your success as you honor the leaders around you! "The wise will hear and increase their learning, and the person of understanding will acquire wise counsel and the skill [to steer his course wisely and lead others to the truth]" (Prov. 1:5, AMP).

You must start moving toward extraordinary people. Make a habit of pursuing greatness. Purchase any book or attend every class that contains new insights to push you forward in your leadership capacity. Take the initiative to introduce yourself to leaders you admire. When you meet successful leaders, reach out to them by being generous with your words of appreciation for their hard work. To set yourself into their awareness, give them a token of gratitude to honor the example they are setting for others to follow. What you respect will come toward you. What you don't respect moves away from you. Honor draws others toward you.

Keep growing as a leader. God has clearly called you to be a person of influence. How do I know? I know because it takes someone like you with vision and courage to submit yourself to this risky role of being a woman leader. As happens with any great leader, the time could come when you might be misunderstood, criticized, even persecuted for pushing ahead. Make change your friend. I once heard someone say, "Change is inevitable, except from a vending machine." Change is coming, so open your mind to new!

Don't give up. Put yourself on a program where you consistently read books and attend conferences that stretch you. Continue to find other leaders who will mentor you. The only way to become the kind of leader people want to follow is to keep growing and learning about leadership. As you desire to expand your leadership in your life, start by asking God to give it to you. Your future will be determined by the questions you continue to ask. Those questions will influence the results you will see. Keep on asking. Keep on knocking.

CHOOSE ADVENTURE

Stuart Brown, a medical doctor, psychiatrist, and founder of the National Institute for Play, says that *play*, not necessity, is the mother of invention. And play isn't just for kids. Engaging in activities, like playing with young children, is as important as diet and exercise in fostering longevity. When we stop playing, we stop developing, and when that happens, the law of entropy takes over—things fall apart. When we stop playing, we start dying.[3]

When you see life as an adventure, your hopes and dreams are never more than a day away! Paul Tillich wrote, "He who risks and fails can be forgiven. But he who never risks and never fails is a failure in his own being." The greatest risk is taking no risks at all. Stay exciting! If your ministry is boring, perhaps it's because you are boring. You must get a life outside of your safety zone where everything is predictable and risk free. In John 10:10, Jesus said, "I came that they may have life and have it abundantly" (ESV).

BUILDING WITH THE END IN MIND

Character is always moving and changing. There's no way we can predict the challenges we'll face in our lives, and usually our priorities will change as we go on. If you desire to be an effective leader but you freak out when you think someone stole your parking spot, or when a child spills her milk, or when your husband does what he wants to do after you disagree with him . . . it won't work. Authenticity and transparency are paramount to build trust in your leadership and to help your team adapt to change.[4]

Remember, zigging and zagging is expected on your leadership journey. Women leaders must adapt to the twists and turns on the road of new opportunities and new obstacles. If you don't change professionally and personally, you can lose perspective and become too rigid to bring value to your mission. From time to time, make the conscious choice to reframe your life and your thinking. Review your goals and consider whether you should change them. Your success strategies from the past may not work for you now. Always be open to change.

Positivity is *key*! Choose an affirmation and say it often to keep you on target. This is my personal affirmation:

I believe I am always guided.
I believe I will always go in the right direction.
I believe God will always make a way when there is no way.

Make your affirmation meaningful to you. It should inspire you to live out the greatness you already have inside you. I look forward to seeing how you are going to change your world!

The World Needs [women]

who cannot be bought;

whose word is their bond;

who put character above wealth;

who possess opinions and a will;

who are larger than their vocations,

who do not hesitate to take chances,

who will not lose their individuality in a crowd;

who will be as honest in small things as in great things;

who will make no compromise with wrong;

whose ambitions are not confined to their own selfish desires;

who will not say they do it because "everybody else does it";

who are true to their friends through good report and evil report, in adversity as well as prosperity;

who do not believe that shrewdness, cunning and hardheadedness are the best qualities for winning success,

who are not ashamed or afraid to stand for the truth when it is unpopular; who can say *"no"* with emphasis, although all the rest of the world says "yes."[5]

EPILOGUE

You have finished this book! What did you read? You read a series of practical and workable strategies for being a successful leader. You also read a formula of belief and practice that, when applied with effort and diligence, will help you win victory over every defeat. I hope the stories demonstrate that you can obtain the same results! However, reading isn't enough. Now it's time to review and persistently practice each strategy in this book. Keep at it until you reach your goals.

I wrote this book out of a sincere desire to coach you forward in your leadership life. It will give me great happiness to know the book has helped you. I have absolute confidence and belief in the principles and strategies outlined. They have been tested in the laboratory of spiritual experience and practical demonstration. They work when worked.

We may never meet in person, but through this book I've had the pleasure of being your ministry leadership coach. We are spiritual friends—forever. I pray for you. God will help you, so believe because God has already empowered you to *lead the way forward.*

NOTES

CHAPTER 1

1. "Stained glass ceiling," Dictionary.com, accessed August 1, 2016, http://www.dictionary.com/browse/stained-glass--ceiling

2. "Glass ceiling," BusinessDictionary.com, accessed August 1, 2016, http://www.businessdictionary.com/definition/glass-ceiling.html

3. Carol Morrison, *The Glass Ceiling* (St. Petersburg, FL: Human Resource Institute, 2005).

4. Chrissie Long, "Women, Leadership and the 'Glass Cliff': Research Roundup" Journalist's Resource, last modified July 17, 2014, accessed June 23, 2016, http://journalistsresource.org/studies/society/gender-society/women-leadership-glass-cliff-research-roundup

5. Daryll Dash, "God Dreams," Dashhouse, last modified January 5, 2016, accessed June 14, 2016, http://dashhouse.com/201611god-dreams/

6. Anthony Robbins, *Ultimate Edge Success Journal* (San Diego, CA: Robbins Research International, Inc., 2012, http://ultimate-edge.s3.amazonaws.com/inner-strength-success-journal.pdf

CHAPTER 2

1. Joyce Meyer, *I Dare You: Embrace Life with Passion* (New York: Faith Words, 2007), vii.

2. Darlene Zschech, *Extravagant Worship* (Bloomington, MN: Bethany House, 2001), 148.

3. John Bevere, *A Heart Ablaze: Igniting a Passion for God* (Nashville: Thomas Nelson, 1999), 14.

4. Meyer, *I Dare You*, 5.

5. Ibid., 10.

6. Bevere, *A Heart Ablaze*, 14.

7. Sheila Weller, "Suddenly That Summer," *Vanity Fair*, last modified July 2012, http://www.vanityfair.com/culture/2012/07/lsd-drugs-summer-of-love-sixties, accessed June 23, 2016

8. Leonard Sweet, *Summoned to Lead* (Grand Rapids: Zondervan, 2004), 13.

9. Ibid., 14.

10. Bevere, *A Heart Ablaze*, 14.

11. Gary McIntosh and Samuel D. Rima, Sr., *Overcoming the Dark Side of Leadership: The Paradox of Personal Dysfunction* (Grand Rapids: Baker Books, 1997), 14.

12. Ibid., 12.

13. Creflo A. Dollar, *8 Steps to Create the Life You Want: The Anatomy of a Successful Life* (New York: FaithWords, 2008), 81.

CHAPTER 3

1. Ken Blanchard and Phil Hodges, *Lead Like Jesus: Lessons from the Greatest Leadership Role Model of All Time* (Nashville: Thomas Nelson, 2008), 4.

2. Warren G. Bennis and Robert J. Thomas, *Leading for a Lifetime: How Defining Moments Shape Leaders of Today and Tomorrow* (Boston: Harvard Business Review Press, 2007), 17.

3. Kevin Kruse, "What Is Leadership," *Forbes*, last modified April 9, 2013, http://www.forbes.com/sites/kevinkruse/2013/04/09/what-is-leadership/#3f6cf7c713e1, accessed July 2016.

4. Ibid.

5. Steve Ogne and Tim Roehl, *TransforMissional Coaching: Empowering Leaders in a Changing Ministry World* (Nashville: B&H Publishing Group, 2008), 30.

6. Ibid., 7.

7. Mind Tools, Ltd. "What Is Leadership," Mind Tools: Essential Tools for an Excellent Career, accessed January 2016, https://www.mindtools.com/pages/article/newLDR_41.htm

8. Blanchard and Hodges, *Lead Like Jesus*, 4.

9. Bennis and Thomas, *Leading*, 142.

10. Ibid., 17.

11. Bernard M. Bass, *The Bass Handbook of Leadership: Theory, Research, and Managerial Applications* (New York: Free Press, 2008), 4.

12. Ibid.

13. Ibid.

14. Ava Oleson, "Bridging the Gap: A Seminar to Attract Female Ministers to Become Credentialed with The Assemblies of God," (DMin project, Assemblies of God Theological Seminary, 2011), 21.

15. Lee G. Bolman and Terrence E. Deal, *Reframing Organizations: Artistry, Choice, and Leadership* (San Francisco: Jossey-Bass, 2008), 377.

16. Bertrand Russell, quoted in Stuart Crainer, *The Ultimate Book of Business Quotations* (Oxford: Capstone Publishing, 1997), 258.

PART 1

1. A special thanks to Keith and Sheila Craft. Their friendship and ministry have greatly impacted my life. Keith and Sheila's teaching on elevated thinking and servant leadership have helped shape my ministry. See http://keithcraft.org

CHAPTER 4

1. Disabled World, "Human Brain Facts and Answers," Disabled World Towards Tomorrow, accessed May 2016, http://www.disabled-world.com/artman/publish/brain-facts.shtml

2. Ibid.

3. Rick Warren, "You Are Not an Accident," CBN, http://www1.cbn.com/devotions/You-Are-Not-an-Accident, accessed May 2016.

4. Rick Warren, "Who Is God's Favorite?" Pastor Rick's Daily Hope, last modified May 21, 2014, accessed August, 2016, http://pastorrick.com/devotional/english/who-is-god-s-favorite.

5. Jenni Catron, *Clout: Discover and Unleash Your God-Given Influence* (Nashville: Nelson Books, 2014), xxi.

CHAPTER 5

1. Alister McGrath, *Christian Theology: An Introduction* (New York: John Wiley & Sons, 2011), 349.

2. Stanley Horton, *Putting Amazing Back into Grace: Embracing the Heart of the Gospel* (Grand Rapids: Baker Books, 2002), 16.

3. Edward W. Younkins, "Capitalism & Commerce: Aristotle, Human Flourishing, and the Limited State," *Le Québécois Libre,* last modified November 22, 2003, accessed July 2016, http://www. quebecoislibre.org/032211-11.htm

CHAPTER 6

1. Project Heaven on Earth, "The 3 Heaven on Earth Questions," Project Heaven on Earth, accessed June 2016, http://www. projectheavenonearth.com/?page_id=49

2. Laurie Beth Jones, *The Path: Creating Your Mission Statement for Work and for Life* (New York: Hyperion, 1998), 4.

CHAPTER 7

1. LIFE *Learning Is for Everyone*, Support and remediation for students with documented learning challenges, see http:// wherelifehappens.org/academic//

2. For more about our ministry in Miami, see Rich Wilkerson and Robyn Wilkerson, *Inside Out: How Everyday People Become Extraordinary Leaders* (Springfield, MO: Salubris Resources, 2015).

3. Sanda Kaufman, Michael Elliott, Deborah Shmueli, "Frames, Framing and Reframing," September 2003, http://pitchanything. com/wp-content/uploads/_pdfs/pitch%20anything%20 companion%20material-frames%20framing%20and%20 reframing.pdf, accessed July 2016.

4. Katherine Ellison, "Being Honest About the Pygmalion Effect," *Discover,* last modified October 29, 2015, http://discovermagazine. com/2015/dec/14-great-expectations, accessed June 2016.

5. Alix Spiegel, "Teacher Expectations Can Influence How Students Perform," NPR, last modified September 2012,

http://www.npr.org/sections/health-shots/2012/09/18/1611 59263/ teachers-expectations-can-influence-how-students-perform, accessed June 2016.

6. R. Rosenthal and S. L. Jacobson, "Teachers' Expectancies: Determinates of Pupils' IQ gains," *Psychological Reports,* 19 (1966), 115–118, http://homepages.gac.edu/~jwotton2/PSY225/ rosenthal66.pdf

7. Ibid., 116.

8. Robert L. Sandidge and Anne C. Ward, "Reframing," in *Quality Performance in Human Services Leadership: Leadership, Values, and Vision,* eds. James F. Gardner and Sylvia Nudler (Baltimore, MD: Brookes Publishing, 1999), 201–21.

9. Viktor E. Frankl, *Man's Search for Meaning* (Boston: Beacon Press, 2006).

10. Ibid., 113.

11. Corrie ten Boom, *The Hiding Place* (Old Tappan, NJ: Bantam Books, 1974), 197–199.

12. Ron Breazeale, "'Positive Reframing' as Optimistic Thinking," *Psychology Today,* last modified September 25, 2012, https:// www.psychologytoday.com/blog/in-the-face-adversity/201209/ positive-reframing-optimistic-thinking, accessed June 2016.

CHAPTER 8

1. Ian Jones, Kirsty Thorpe, and Janet Wootton, eds., *Women and Ordination in the Christian Churches: International Perspectives* (London: Bloomsbury Publishing, 2008).

2. Joy C. Charlton, "Revisiting Gender and Religion," *Review of Religious Research* 57 3 (2015): 331–39.

3. Mary Jo Neitz, "Becoming Visible: Religion and Gender in Sociology," *Sociology of Religion* (2014): 58.

4. Sabine Losch, Eva Traut-Mattausch, Maximilian D. Mühlberger, and Eva Jonas, "Comparing the Effectiveness of Individual Coaching, Self-Coaching, and Group Training: How Leadership Makes the Difference," *Frontiers in Psychology* 7 (2016).

5. Tim Theeboom, Bianca Beersma, Annelies E. M. van Vianen, "Does Coaching Work?—A Meta-Analysis on the Effects of Coaching on Individual Level Outcomes in an Organizational Context," *The Journal of Positive Psychology*, 1–18, http://www.coachfederation. org/files/FileDownloads/173-A%20Meta-analysis%20on%20 the%20Effects%20of%20Coaching%20on%20Individual.pdf

6. Luke Mastin, "Age Associated Memory Impairment," The Human Memory, accessed June 2016, http://www.human-memory.net/ disorders_age.html

7. Siegrid Löwel and W. Singer, "Selection of Intrinsic Horizontal Connections in the Visual Cortex by Correlated Neuronal Activity," *United States: American Association for the Advancement of Science* 255, January 10, 1992, 209–12.

8. John R. Hughes, "Post-Tetanic Potentiation," *Physiological Reviews* 38 (1), 1958: 91–113.

9. Caroline Leaf, *Who Switched Off My Brain?: Controlling Toxic Thoughts and Emotions* (Nashville: Thomas Nelson, 2009), 3.

10. Christof Koch and Patricia Kuhl, "Decoding 'the Most Complex Object in the Universe,'" last modified June 14, 2013, http://www. npr.org/2013/06/14/191614360/decoding-the-most-complex- object-in-the-universe, accessed June 2016.

11. Daniel J. Siegel, *Mindsight: The New Science of Personal Transformation* (New York: Bantam Books, 2010), 39.

12. Katherine A. Kaplan, "College Faces Mental Health Crisis," The Harvard Crimson Online, July 12, 2004, http://www.thecrimson. com/article/2004/1/12/college-faces-mental-health-crisis-one/, accessed June 2016.

13. Robert Biswas-Diener and Ben Dean, *Positive Psychology Coaching: Putting the Science of Happiness to Work for Your Clients* (Hoboken, NJ: John Wiley & Sons, 2010), 14.

14. David G. Myers and Ed Diener, "Who Is Happy?" *Psychological Science* 6, 1 (1995): 10–19.

15. Sonja Lyubomirsky, Laura King, and Ed Diener, "The Benefits of Frequent Positive Affect: Does Happiness Lead to Success?"

Psychological Bulletin 131.6 (2005): 803.

16. Bennis and Nanus, *Leaders: Strategies for Taking Charge* (San Francisco: Harper Paperbacks, 2003), 36.

17. Ibid., 36.

18. Dollar, *8 Steps to Create the Life You Want*, 34.

19. Eleanor Longden, *Learning from the Voices in My Head*, TED Books Book 39, (N.P.: Kindle Publishing, 2013).

20. Ibid.

21. Eleanor Longden, Dirk Corstens, Sandra Escher, and Marius Romme, "Voice Hearing in a Biographical Context: A Model for Formulating the Relationship Between Voices and Life History," *Psychosis: Psychological, Social and Integrative Approaches*, vol. 4 (3), 2012, 224–34.

22. Longden, *Learning from the Voices in My Head*.

CHAPTER 10

1. "To Lead," Google, accessed July 2016, https://www.google.com/#q=define+%22to+lead%22

2. Center for Creative Leadership "Leading Effectively," Center for Creative Leadership, last modified 2005, accessed May 15, 2016, http://www.ccl.org/leadership/pdf/landing/20042005Final.pdf#_ga=1.258282703.413867053.1463235013, 38.

3. Ibid.

4. K. E. Khan, S. E. Kahn, and A. G. Chaudhry, "Impact of Servant Leadership on Workplace Spirituality: Moderating Role of Involvement Culture," *Pakistan Journal of Science* 67, no. 1 (2015): 110.

5. Ibid.

6. Ibid.

7. Ibid.

8. John Maxwell, *Failing Forward: Turning Mistakes into Stepping Stones for Success* (Nashville: Thomas Nelson, 2000), 156.

9. Ibid.

10. Ibid.

11. Ibid.

12. Dino Rizzo, *Servolution: Starting a Church Revolution Through Serving* (Grand Rapids: Zondervan, 2009), 26.

13. Kenneth C. Haugk, *Antagonists in the Church: How to Identify and Deal with Destructive Conflict* (Minneapolis: Augsburg, 1988), 25.

14. Craig E. Runde and Tim A. Flanagan, *Becoming a Conflict Competent Leader: How You and Your Organization Can Manage Conflict Effectively* (San Francisco: Jossey-Bass, 2007), 35.

15. Ken Sande, *The Peacemaker: A Biblical Guide to Resolving Personal Conflict*, 3rd ed. (Grand Rapids: Baker, 2004), 87.

16. Ibid., 49.

17. Dallas Willard, *Renovation of the Heart* (Colorado Springs, CO: NavPress, 2002), 30.

18. Bennis and Nanus, *Leaders,* 36.

19. Jennifer J. Deal, Marian Ruderman, Sarah Stawiski, William Gentry, Laura Graves, and Todd Weber, "Building Trust in the Workplace: A Key to Retaining Women," The Center for Creative Leadership, accessed May 24, 2016, http://media.ccl.org/wp-content/uploads/2015/02/BuildingTrustInTheWorkplace.pdf#_ga =1.126317198.2052048082.1469765326.

20. Ibid.

CHAPTER 11

1. Rizzo, *Servolution*, 48.

2. Leighton Ford, *Transforming Leadership: Jesus' Way of Creating Vision, Shaping Values & Empowering Change* (Downers Grove, IL: IVP Books, 1993), 153.

3. Ibid.

4. Ibid., 166.

5. Ibid., 187.

CHAPTER 13

1. Scott Williams, "Self-Awareness and Personal Development," Wright State University, accessed July 25, 2016, http://www.wright.

edu/~scott.williams/LeaderLetter/selfawareness.htm

2. Phil Munsey, *Legacy Now: Why Everything About You Matters* (Lake Mary, FL: Charisma House, 2008), 187.

3. Ibid.

4. Stuart Friedman, "Setting and Getting to Your Goal," Progressive Management Associates, accessed July 24, 2016, http://pma-co.com/setting-and-getting-to-your-goal/

CHAPTER 14

1. James T. Bradford, *Lead So Others Can Follow: 12 Practices and Principles for Ministry* (Springfield, MO: Salubris Resources, 2015).

2. Samantha P. Lumbert, "Conformity and Group Mentality: Why We Comply," Personality Research, last modified 2005, http://www.personalityresearch.org/papers/lumbert.removed

3. J. D. Bozarth, "Quantum Theory and the Person-Centered Approach." *Journal of Counseling & Development*, 64 (1985): 179–82. doi:10.1002/j.1556–6676.1985.tb01066.x

4. Jennifer G. Hickey, "Pew: Only 46 Percent of US Families Are 'Traditional,'" Newsmax, January 16, 2015, http://www.newsmax.com/US/Family-single-parent-children-Pew-Research/2015/01/16/id/619047/, accessed May 2014.

5. National Women's Law Center, "National Snapshot: Poverty Among Women & Families, 2014," NWLC, last modified September 17, 2015, https://nwlc.org/resources/national-snapshot-poverty-among-women-families-2014/, accessed May 2015.

6. Mark Mather, "U.S. Children in Single Mother Families," PBR, last modified May 2010, http://www.prb.org/pdf10/single-motherfamilies.pdf, accessed February 2013.

7. David Francis, "Why Do Women Outnumber Men in College?" NBER, accessed July 15, 2016, http://www.nber.org/digest/jan07/w12139.html

8. National Women's Law Center, "NWLC Analysis of 2014 Census Poverty Data," NWLC, last modified October 21, 2015, https://nwlc.org/resources/nwlc-analysis-2014-census-poverty-data/, accessed May 2015.

9. S. Alexander Haslam, Stephen D. Reicher, and Michael J. Platow. *The New Psychology of Leadership: Identity, Influence and Power* (East Sussex: Psychology Press, 2010), 18.

10. Nancy Beach, *Gifted to Lead: The Art of Leading as a Woman in the Church* (Grand Rapids: Zondervan, 2008), 123.

11. Ibid.

12. Joanna Barsh, Josephine Mogelof, and Caroline Webb, "How Centered Leaders Achieve Extraordinary Results," *McKinsey Quarterly*, last modified October 2010, accessed May 16, 2016, http://www.mckinsey.com/global-themes/leadership/how-centered-leaders-achieve-extraordinary-results

CHAPTER 16

1. Andries van Heerden, "What's Transformation?" Emmanel Church, accessed May 24, 2016, http://www.emmanuellife.org/churchlife/media/transformation/index.html

2. Greg Ogden, *Transforming Discipleship* (Downers Grove, IL: InterVarsity Press, 2003), 103.

CHAPTER 17

1. Alyssa C.D. Cheadle and Loren L. Toussaint. "Forgiveness and Physical Health in Healthy Populations." *Forgiveness and Health*. Springer Netherlands, 2015. 91–106.

2. Loren Toussaint, et al. "Effects of Lifetime Stress Exposure on Mental and Physical Health in Young Adulthood: How Stress Degrades and Forgiveness Protects Health," *Journal of Health Psychology* 21.6 (2016): 1004–14.

3. Susan Nolen-Hoeksema, "Gender Differences in Depression." *Current Directions in Psychological Science* 10, 5 (2001): 173–76.

4. Kelley Holland, "Working Moms Still Take on Bulk of Household Chores," CNBC, last modified April 28, 2015, http://www.cnbc.com/2015/04/28/me-is-like-leave-it-to-beaver.html, accessed may 2016.

5. Institute for Employment Studies, "Report summary: Working

Long Hours: a Review of the Evidence, Volume 1 – Main Report," IES, accessed June 24, 2015, http://www.employment-studies. co.uk/report-summaries/report-summary-working-long-hours-review-evidence-volume-1-%E2%80%93-main-report

6. Claire Cain Miller, "Stressed, Tired, Rushed: A Portrait of the Modern Family," *The New York Times*, last modified November 4, 2015, http://www.nytimes.com/2015/11/05/upshot/stressed-tired-rushed-a-portrait-of-the-modern-family.html?_r=0, accessed May 2016.

7. Kate Irby, "Men Work Longer Hours Than Women and Women Do More Housework, Report Finds," McClatchy D C, last modified June 27, 2016, http://www.mcclatchydc.com/news/politics-government/article86173192.html#storylink=cpy, accessed July 2016.

8. Kelly Clay, "Why Millennial Women Are Burning Out," *Fast Company*, last modified March 8, 2016, http://www.fastcompany.com/3057545/the-future-of-work/why-millennial-women-are-burning-out

9. Chen-Bo Zhong, Ap Dijksterhuis, and Adam D. Galinsky, "The Merits of Unconscious Thought in Creativity," *Psychological Science* 19, 9 (2008): 912–18.

CONCLUSION

1. Jim Collins and Morten T. Hansen, *Great by Choice: Uncertainty, Chaos, and Luck* (New York: Harper Collins, 2010), 1.

2. Dawn Chere Wilkerson and Rich Wilkerson Jr., Vous Church, http://vouschurch.com/

3. Stuart L. Brown, *Play: How It Shapes the Brain, Opens the Imagination, and Invigorates the Soul* (New York: Penguin Group, 2009), 72–73.

4. Linda Miller and Jane Creswell, *Beginners Guide to Christian Coaching: How to Have Powerful Conversations That Really Make a Difference* (N.P.: Coach Approach Ministries, 2005), https://coachapproachministries.org/beginners-guide-sign-up/

5. Unpublished pamphlet quoted by Ted Wilhelm Engstrom, *The Making of a Christian Leader* (Grand Rapids: Zondervan, 1976), 120.

ABOUT THE AUTHOR

Robyn Wilkerson received her call to ministry at the age of twelve through a series of life-changing encounters with God. Since then she has led multiple ministries, raised four sons who are in ministry, and currently copastors Trinity Church in Miami, Florida, with her husband, Rich Wilkerson.

Robyn completed her doctor of ministry degree from Evangel University in 2017, focusing on coaching and women in leadership. Her formal education and her personal experiences allow her to coach individuals to help them grow and succeed in their personal and professional lives. Over the years, Robyn has personally experienced the difficulties women leaders face, and she wants to use every resource at her disposal to guide other women leaders as they strive to reach their full potential.

Robyn's gift for teaching and her flare for staying on the cutting edge of ministry make her tremendously effective in all aspects of ministry— including teaching, preaching, and the administration of a cross-cultural, faith-based, social service ministry. The God-given gift Robyn possesses for teaching the Bible has flourished through television appearances and speaking engagements. Her energetic and passionate style of ministry fervently declares God's Word and its power to change lives.

Robyn's professional career has spanned many varied industries, including mortgage banking, residential construction, television production, and nonprofit administration. She is a speaker, preacher, and professional life coach.

Robyn and Rich, married for forty years, have four sons, three daughters-in-law, and three beautiful grandbabies. Robyn is coauthor of *Inside Out: How Everyday People Become Extraordinary Leaders!*

FOR MORE INFORMATION

For more information about this and other valuable resources, please visit

WWW.MYHEALTHYCHURCH.COM